GLIMPSES OF THE
ANCIENT
SOUTHWEST

Pueblo Bonito at Chaco Canyon, ca. 1937-47. Photograph by Ferenz Fedor. (Neg. no. 101956, courtesy Museum of New Mexico.)

GLIMPSES OF THE
ANCIENT
SOUTHWEST

BY DAVID E. STUART

ANCIENT CITY PRESS
SANTA FE, NEW MEXICO

International Standard Book Number
Paperback 0-941270-21-1
Cloth Library Edition 0-941270-22-X

Library of Congress Catalogue Number
85-070118

Third Printing

Designed by Mary Powell
Cover photograph by Cynthia M. Stuart

Typesetting by Composing Services
Tularosa, New Mexico
Printed in the United States of America
by Guynes Printing Co. of New Mexico, Inc.
Albuquerque, New Mexico

FOR

Avis and John
Frances and Cynthia

Four who have watched over me
both in good times and in bad.

Three Corn Ruin: a Navajo and Pueblo ruin of the early eighteenth century.
Drawing by Scott Andrae.

TABLE OF CONTENTS

PREFACE

Four years ago this month I was busy putting the finishing touches on another book, *Prehistoric New Mexico*, written with my friend and assistant, Rory Gauthier. Two editions of that work have already been well-received by the scholarly community, both as a technical reference and as a textbook. However, unlike this present book of essays, its completion brought me little joy. Let me explain.

The *Prehistoric New Mexico* project was long, very technical, and politically delicate. Bureaucrats were involved, too many of them every bit as authoritarian and tedious as those portrayed in the most outrageous Hollywood comedy sketches. Worse yet, Rory and I had uncovered a remarkably fresh and exciting picture of Southwestern archeology, hidden for many years in the thousands of field data forms tucked away in dozens of institutional, steel file drawers. But it was the politics of our project that initially fascinated our colleagues—not our discoveries. What frustration!

Meanwhile, two friends, Carlos Caraveo and Norman Todd, simultaneously began urging me to write an archeology article or two for local newspapers. At that time Carlos was circulation manager of the *New Mexico Independent* and Norman, an attorney by vocation, also wrote a political column for the *Silver City Enterprise*.

In the 1880s, Adolph Bandelier, the legendary founder of Southwestern archeology, wrote regularly for the newspapers. In fact, the Eastern press provided him an important income for features carrying then exotic datelines like "Santa Fe," "Canyon de los Frijoles," and "Pecos, New Mexico Territory." However, in the intervening century, archeologists turned away from the news reading public and concentrated on the scholarly press—a narrow but prestigious audience.

In January of 1982, after nearly a century of silence, the *Silver City Enterprise* and the *New Mexico Independent* again carried newspaper articles written for the general public by a professional anthropologist. Public response was immediate—within a few days both papers asked me how they could regularly carry my "column." Tongue-in-cheek, I named it

"New Mexico's Heritage" and kept on writing, expecting interest to fade. But it did not. Today, fourteen papers carry the series, from Raton and Farmington in the north to Las Cruces and Silver City in the south. The editors of New Mexico's newspapers, particularly small town ones, are generally a friendly and progressive lot. Therefore, many of the essays in this collection were first written at the special request of one or another local paper. Some wisely lobbied me not to neglect tales about the people and places important to me in my everyday job. So I have written about friends like John Broster and Rory Gauthier, with whom I walked so many long, tiring miles in New Mexico's "back country." I have written about John Beardsley too, although we have other memories. I have also told you about Frank Broilo, who died too young.

Articles about the new and exciting picture of New Mexico's past that Rory and I so tediously weeded out of "dead" files are also included. They are as accurate as those I write for textbooks, but much more fun to write. I hope they also bring you pleasure. If you enjoy this book, want to know more, or have knowledge to share, write to me through the publisher.

While I have selected articles as informative as space permits, this collection does not constitute a textbook approach to our region's past. These essays are genuinely what the title says, absorbing "Glimpses of the Ancient Southwest."

Albuquerque   David Edward Stuart
November 1984

ACKNOWLEDGMENTS

I am a fortunate man—not in riches, but in the richness of my friends and mentors. Most of these essays were first typed by Louise Weishaupt of Albuquerque. Without Louise, my "New Mexico's Heritage" newspaper series would never get to editors across the state. Gail Wimberly, of Composing Services in Tularosa, is special too. She has composed my most important book projects, and I hope there will be many more. I also want to thank Cynthia Stuart, Tracey Morse, Rory Gauthier, Scott Andrae, John Stein, and Leonard Raab for helping me with photographs and artwork. All of the book's photographs were carefully hand processed by Scott Caraway in Albuquerque. Mary Powell and Marta Weigle, my publishers, have been both patient and supportive.

Not a few newspaper and magazine editors have taken a special, and important, interest in my work. These include Rick Phillips and Mike Cook, formerly of the *Silver City Enterprise*, Ellen Syvertson of the *Valencia County News Bulletin*, David Mullings of the *Raton Range*, Scott Sandlin of the *Farmington Daily Times*, Mark Acuff of the *New Mexico Independent*, Reed Eckhardt of the *Gallup Independent*, James McCaffrey of the *Rio Rancho Observer*, and Patrick Beckett, publisher of the journal *New Mexico Archaeology and History*.

I especially want to thank V. B. "Barrett" Price, former editor of *Century* magazine and now editor of *New Mexico Magazine*. Barrett, an excellent writer himself, takes special pains to encourage and compliment other writers. Without him, several of the finest essays in this volume would not have been written.

And I need to thank Tony Hillerman too. Tony is one of my favorite writers, so I jumped at the chance to take his "Persuasive Writing" class at the University of New Mexico in the spring of 1984. I felt somewhat out of place with all those young journalism students, but I did improve my writing. During class, Tony suggested revisions in a number of these essays. Several pieces are considerably stronger as a result.

Others helped in important ways. Many friends and regular readers of my articles, both at U.N.M. and around the state, filled out questionnaires about their favorite essays and possible book titles, then sent them back to me. I weighed this advice heavily and am grateful for their suggestions. Finally, although not every essay in this book has previously been published, many have appeared in the following publications prior to revision. I want to thank each of them for making my work available to the public: *Century Magazine*, *Southwest Heritage Magazine*, *New Mexico Archaeology and History*, *New Mexico Magazine*, *The Sundial*, *New Mexico Independent*, *Sandoval County Times Independent*, *Silver City Enterprise*, *Farmington Daily Times*, *Gallup Independent*, *Las Vegas Daily Optic*, *Raton Range*, *Union County Leader*, *Valencia County News Bulletin*, *New Mexico Daily Lobo*, *Las Cruces Bulletin*, *Silver City Daily Press*, *Hobbs Daily News Sun*, *Lincoln County News*, *DeBaca County News*, *Jicarilla Chieftain*, *Socorro Defensor-Chieftain*, and the *Rio Rancho Observer*, currently "home" newspaper to the "New Mexico's Heritage" series.

PART I

A LAND RICH IN ARCHEOLOGICAL HERITAGE

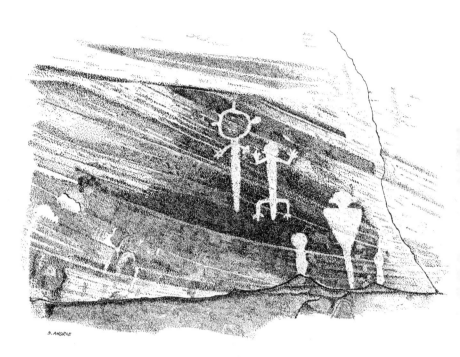

Anasazi petroglyphs. Drawing by Scott Andrae.

The American Southwest is a vast domain. More than thirty thousand archeological sites have been found in New Mexico alone—a state larger than Maine, Massachusetts, Connecticut, Vermont, New Hampshire, Rhode Island, New York, New Jersey, and Delaware combined! Nowhere else in the United States are the ancient and the modern so intricately interwoven into a distinctive regional society.

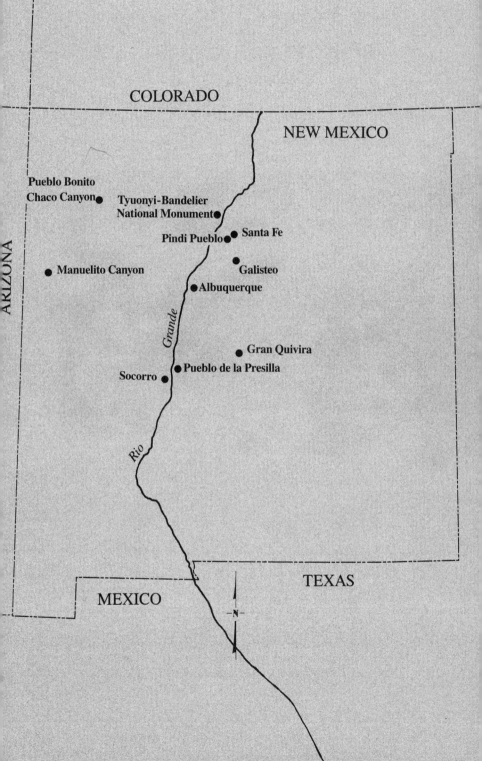

Pueblo de la Presilla is a series of large masonry room-blocks arranged around a flat, rectangular plaza. They have gradually fallen into long irregular mounds of rock and soil. Clumps of creosote and grasses invade the square. This decay happens slowly, but there has been enough time. The plaza was last swept to make ready for dances nearly 650 years ago.

A gentle current of air rises from the Rio Grande more than a hundred feet below. Socorro, New Mexico, lies due west, across the river. There, the morning sun shimmers on galvanized roofs and warms adobe walls, the color of fine old meerschaum. The breeze whispers the call of a magpie from the tangle of cottonwoods and sunflowers along the river.

Pueblo de la Presilla also has another name. It is LA 31720. That number is something special.

Just over half a century ago, LA 1, Pindi Pueblo near Santa Fe, was entered into the records of the Museum of New Mexico's Laboratory of Anthropology. It has taken survey archeologists that long to record the more than thirty thousand known archeological sites in New Mexico. Thirty thousand prehistoric sites is an impressive number, and today we know a great deal more about New Mexico's past than did our colleagues who walked survey so long ago. But much work still remains to be done, for only a small portion of New Mexico has been walked foot by foot.

New Mexico is a vast domain. It contains over 121,000 square miles, nearly 80 million acres. It is larger than Maine, Massachusetts, Connecticut, Vermont, New Hampshire, Rhode Island, New York, New Jersey and Delaware combined! If one hundred top-notch survey teams of four archeologists each started tomorrow, we would know how many sites there were in all of New Mexico by about the middle of the next century.

I doubt that the job will ever be done. New Mexico has approximately enough archeologists to field forty trained field survey crews, no more. About half of these 160 archeologists work for universities or federal and state agencies. Most of their time is taken up with teaching or administrative

Pueblo Colorado in the Galisteo Basin. Photograph by Rory P. Gauthier.

paperwork, so they get to do little fieldwork. In other words, we really have perhaps twenty field crews available to do the basic job of site survey, but on any given day in New Mexico fewer than ten crews are actually in the field. There is no one to pay the wages of the others, unemployment runs about fifty percent year in and year out. Most do well to get six to eight months' work each year. The standard rate is a flat $65.00 a day, no insurance, no retirement, no annual leave—$65.00 a day, period. That's what a university degree, an eye for detail, and a good pair of legs is worth. Most years that averages out to about $8,000 to $10,000. If you break your leg or get "snake bit," that's your problem. The ones who stick with it are quite skilled and very, very dedicated.

A top-notch crew of four can survey and record archeological material found in about 160 acres per day. About two days of laboratory analysis and write-up are required for each day spent in the field. In the decade from 1970 to

1980, an average of 120,000 acres was surveyed in New Mexico every year (10 crews x 75 field days each year), and an average of 2,000 sites per year were entered into the files at the State Museum—one site for every 60 acres covered. The thirty-two thousand archeological sites recorded at the State Museum represent just under two million acres of survey coverage in half a century—*one-fortieth* of the State of New Mexico. It has taken 50 years to do a mere 2½ *percent* of the job of rediscovering New Mexico's past. At that rate, it would take *two thousand years* to find and record the rest. Actually, this is overly pessimistic, for only an average of 200 sites per year were recorded in Santa Fe in the 40 years from 1930 to 1970—the equivalent of 1,200 acres surveyed per year. At the 1970s' rate of 120,000 acres per year, we could get the job done in just another 624 years.

How many archeological sites would we find if every square inch of New Mexico were surveyed? A conservative estimate would be 500,000. This is conservative because, prior to 1980, all the archeological surveys ever conducted in New Mexico had yielded an average of nine archeological sites per square mile. If this average were to prevail for the unsurveyed parts of the state, there would be more than one million sites in all!

One million is probably too optimistic a figure, for archeologists have been adept at finding the densest concentration of sites. But by no means have all such large "important" sites been discovered long ago. As recently as 1979, major Chacoan sites, some with partially standing walls, were being discovered *within sight of* Interstate 40.

Many of the 30,000-odd sites that have been recorded are not very impressive. Most people would not recognize half of them to be much of anything at all. Hundreds of these might consist of only half a dozen fragments of pottery scattered about. At hundreds more there would be a few flakes of chert or basalt, struck from stone cores long ago, or an ancient hearth of fire-cracked rock eroding from a sand dune.

But others are quite grand: the likes of Pueblo Bonito at Chaco Canyon National Monument, Tyuonyi in Bandelier, and the great stone missions at Quarai and Gran Quivira in the wooded mesas of central New Mexico. Sites like these do capture the imagination. Perhaps for this reason most books on archeology for the general reader are written about just

5

the few dozen very impressive sites that have been excavated and restored for visitors.

However, there are thousands of other archeological sites that can also impress you when you stumble across them unexpectedly, if you learn to understand what they mean. That is what survey archeology is about: thousands of archeological sites—both the great and the small—and what they mean. Often one obscure little site does not yield much information. But when archeologists learn a small fiber of fact from a hundred or a thousand similar ones, a great bundle of scientific threads is slowly piled up. These bundles are the unique creation of the survey archeologist. When they are added to the in-depth information from New Mexico's three hundred excavated sites, they create a very special brush—one that can be used to paint a vivid picture of New Mexico's past.

So, the important treasures of New Mexico's archeology are by no means limited to the small number of sites familiar to the public. Few realize that Manuelito Canyon, tucked away west of Gallup, once nearly became the National Monument, instead of Chaco Canyon. At Manuelito, striking circular towers and crumbling masonry walls still look down on small farm plots, fallow now for 800 years.

Others are not aware that the Galisteo Basin District, just to the southeast of Santa Fe, contains more than a dozen grand pueblos which were founded after the decline of Chaco Canyon. The masonry Pueblo of Shé, with 1,543 ground floor rooms, positively dwarfs the 332 rooms and kivas of the more famous Pueblo Bonito at Chaco Canyon. Another, Pueblo Colorado, with about a thousand rooms, is not far behind.

Although not all important sites are so large, New Mexico's collection of archeological "Crown Jewels" is both immense and stunning. The time has come to fling open the doors to our vault—and show the world these treasures.

Left: The Mission of San Buenaventura at Gran Quivira National Monument. Photograph by Leonard Raab.

Few citizens realize that from an upper-floor window in almost any of Albuquerque's office buildings one can look out over lands that have been lived in for at least twelve thousand years—a span of six hundred human generations. Even fewer Albuquerqueans realize that many of their homes sit on the residue of those six hundred generations. An estimated seven thousand prehistoric sites exist in Bernalillo county, more than sixty percent of them covered by modern Albuquerque.

No one knows when the first nomadic families came because evidence of their passing is scant and difficult to date accurately. However, by 10,000 B.C., Paleo-Indian people of the "Clovis" period inhabited the high mesas around Albuquerque.

Clovis families lived at the very end of the Ice Age, co-existing with mammoth, sabre-toothed tigers, and the formidable dire wolf. They traveled in small family bands, stopping to camp for a few days or weeks, then moved for fresh hunting grounds. Before urban sprawl consumed so much of the city's open lands, their distinctive stone lanceheads occasionally turned up as isolated finds in sandy arroyos or on juniper-studded mesas.

Between 9,000 and 8,000 B.C. the Ice Age climate softened, many animal species became extinct, and herds of giant bison roamed rich grasslands along the Rio Grande. With them came hunters of the "Folsom" period, carrying a sophisticated stone lancehead that was grooved like a bayonet.

Folsom people were relatively numerous, hunting and camping along the high West Mesa between Bernalillo and Los Lunas. In fact, the Rio Rancho site, now an area of housing developments, is the only completely excavated Folsom period campsite in North America. Investigated in 1966 and 1967, it yielded a rich array of lanceheads, tools, and traces of two packed earth "floors." These were faint remains of shelters ten thousand to eleven thousand years old—the only Folsom ones ever found!

How large was Albuquerque's population in Folsom times? An estimated dozen family bands, perhaps a hundred

Late prehistoric petroglyphs overlooking Albuquerque's west mesa.
Photograph by Cynthia M. Stuart.

people in all, roamed an area about the size of Bernalillo
County. Three to five of these extended families camped
at the Rio Rancho site. Compared to our own times, the
world was vast and people were few.

Yet others came to Albuquerque. Eventually, the giant
bison vanished, it became warmer and drier, and larger herds
of smaller bison filled eastern New Mexico's grasslands. With
them, about 6,500 B.C., came buffalo hunters of the "Cody"
period, armed with long, thin "Eden" lanceheads. These
dagger-like stone blades were wicked stabbing tools.

Group kills of a hundred bison or more took place on the
eastern plains, ample testimony both to the skill of Cody
hunters and to their technological efficiency. But no large
kill sites have been found in Albuquerque. Here, Cody
hunters probably took less exotic local game like deer from
the West Mesa and elk from the Sandias. Then as now, winters may have been milder in the Albuquerque Basin than in
surrounding areas, drawing families to shelter within sight of
the Sandias.

But the Cody period's severe drying trend had not yet done its worst. By 5,000 B.C., New Mexico was hot and water scarce. Buffalo herds had retreated to the Nation's northern plains, and "Classic" hunting society was transformed into an "Archaic" lifestyle. Foraging for small game and wild plant foods became much more important. Population grew, home territories became smaller, and family camps were longer inhabited.

Local population increased throughout the Archaic period, leaving hundreds of small sites, today marked by bits of flaked stone and piles of fire-cracked cobbles, evidence of cooking activity. Prior to the development of pottery, clay-lined baskets were filled with water, then red hot cobbles were tossed in until food could be boiled. By 1,000 B.C., small-cobbed corn was grown locally, and Bernalillo County's population probably numbered 1,000 to 1,500. Between that time and the birth of Christ, the pace of change increased and population exploded. The general area became thickly settled as small villages of dugout "pithouses" sprang up.

In the thousand years between 500 B.C. and A.D. 500, Albuquerque's West Mesa near Corrales was one of North America's rare crucibles of early village life. Settlements were small, typically two or three pithouses. Pottery was not manufactured locally until about A.D. 400. These early villages depended increasingly on modest harvests of corn, beans, and squash to supplement small game and wild plant foods. Boca Negra Cave, overlooking newly built west-side townhouses, yielded, around A.D. 387, the earliest evidence in New Mexico of a large-cobbed variety of corn—one which undoubtedly doubled or tripled potential harvests.

By A.D. 500, the Albuquerque area—*just as it is today*— was both a crossroads of important trade routes and an amalgam of the several distinctive regional cultures found in western and central New Mexico. Anasazi farmers inhabited northwestern New Mexico and adjacent portions of Colorado, Utah, and Arizona. Mogollon villagers inhabited southwestern New Mexico and portions of Arizona. Turquoise, regional pottery, and ground shell jewelry all passed through the Albuquerque area, as they do still.

In the four hundred years between A.D. 500 and 900, western New Mexico's pithouse villages grew ever larger. Harvests increased, trade intensified, and cultural differences

10

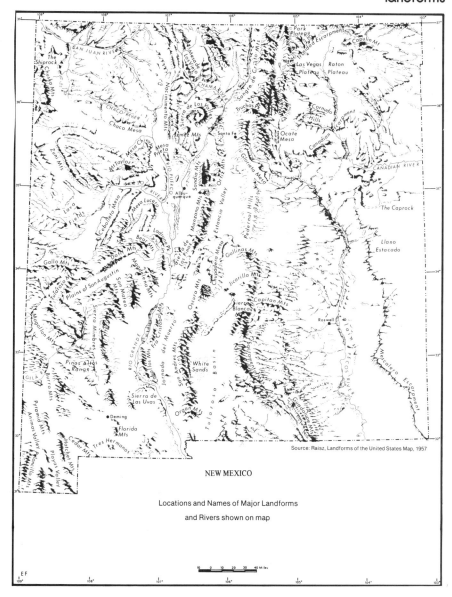

Source: Raisz, Landforms of the United States Map, 1957

NEW MEXICO

Locations and Names of Major Landforms
and Rivers shown on map

Reprinted from *New Mexico in Maps* by Jerry L. Williams and Paul E. McAllister. Copyright 1979 by the Technology Application Center of the University of New Mexico. All rights reserved by The University of New Mexico Press.

11

between the Mogollon and Anasazi became more pronounced. Population increased dramatically in the A.D. 900s and the Albuquerque area, then the eastern frontier of village life, drew new settlers from the Anasazi country to the northwest.

By A.D. 1050, after a century of expansion, Anasazi farmers had created a huge, complex network of roadways and district trading villages. Archeologists refer to this as the "Chaco Phenomenon." Although centered on Chaco Canyon National Monument, 140 miles northwest of Albuquerque, the southeastern corner of the Chacoan frontier ran along the Rio Puerco west of Nine Mile Hill. There, Guadalupe ruin, a huge Chacoan stronghold, still marks the boundary. From it one can easily see the warm glow of Albuquerque's evening lights.

To the south, Mogollon villagers had begun to create the famous Mimbres Period pottery—eventually traded over an area of forty thousand square miles. Both Mimbres pottery and Anasazi bowls, decorated in geometric black-on-white patterns, have been found in ancient village sites within Albuquerque's city limits.

But the fabulous Chaco and Mimbres periods were short-lived. By A.D. 1150 western New Mexico's farmers had abandoned the lowlands and new settlements sprang up in forested highlands. It was during this period that the Sandia and Manzano mountain districts were settled. Today, on Sundays hundreds of Albuquerque's families flock to the Bella Vista, a favorite restaurant in the cool Cedar Crest district east of town. Many of the restaurant's tables overlook rolling hills vegetated by piñon and ponderosa—an area of refuge for Anasazi villagers in the difficult two centuries after Chaco's decline.

By A.D. 1300, an extended drought had forced survivors to settle again along the Rio Grande where, in the mid 1500s, Spanish explorers found many large Pueblos. Two of these, Sandia and Isleta, are still part of greater Albuquerque.

Albuquerque is truly remarkable. For twelve thousand years, every major event in southwestern prehistory left its mark on the city's environs. Think of it! Nearly nine thousand years after Folsom shelters were scooped out of Rio Rancho's brown clay, the first prehistoric settlements were founded in Santa Fe. If charming Santa Fe merits distinction as "The City Different," then Albuquerque, more than five times older, is surely "The City Ancient."

PART II

CLASSIC "HUNTING" SOCIETY

Giant bison skull and Folsom lancehead. Drawing by Scott Andrae.

People were few and the world was vast. From about 10,000 B.C. to 5,000 B.C., small family bands of Paleo-Indians spent entire lifetimes on trek—hunting large game in good times or scouring the landscape for anything edible, plant or animal, in seasons of want.

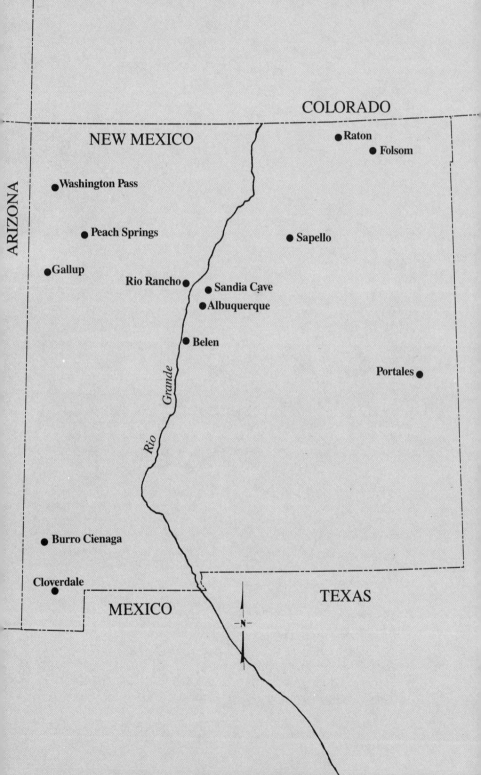

Roads have always crossed at Sapello, north of Las Vegas—
long before the soft sounds of Spanish were first heard on the
old trail to Mora and long before the earliest ancestors of
today's Pueblo Indians settled and farmed in New Mexico.
"Clovis" hunters, the earliest, well-documented Paleo-Indian
people, first came here more than 120 centuries ago.
It is snowing again. An old green pickup slides gently into
the crossroads. There, a ring of tree-studded hills hides an
uneven little valley. Cold wind pours down from the east
face of the Sangre de Cristos and moans along the course of
Sapello Creek, not two yards wide. It glides downstream to
empty rolling plains, now hidden behind a swirling curtain
of snow.

Once similar snows enveloped the bison herds which
formed in the fall along the mountainous edges of the high
plains. Here giant ancestors of the buffalo first drew wander-
ing Paleo-Indian families to the formidable arc of mesas and
sharp hills between Raton and Las Vegas. In this region's
broken terrain, buffalo could be ambushed by men on foot
and driven into bone-shattering ravines and arroyos.

Surrounding hilltops provided hunters with superb early
morning staging areas. As the sun strengthened, warming air
wafted uphill, away from the grasslands. Game could be
observed grazing below, even miles away, but human sight,
sounds, and scent drifted above the reach of animal senses.

From these vantage points some stole downhill to outflank
the herds—stealthy, tedious work. By midday a thin line of
hunters would have begun the drive. Shaggy beasts, manuevered away from the open plateaus and safety, fled uphill
into wide, grassy swales. Soon these narrowed into sinister
little tongues of grassland protruding from the mouths of
ponderosa-studded coves. There the hunts ended.

It took patience, skill, and improbable stamina for men on
foot to break even a small band of monstrous bison. Success
varied. Some years the herds did not appear. But, in good
years, from ten to one hundred animals might be taken at
once. At other times the wind might shift unexpectedly,
stampeding herds alerted by a widening pool of human scent.

An exposed forehead, or one careless movement in the ponderosa could turn the quarry from three hundred yards. Heavy winter snows made tracking simple, and bison might be stranded in deep drifts. But midwinter hunts also involved special risks. Stalking a herd is especially difficult because human scent carries far in snow-moistened air and treacherous gullies are hidden from view. Once the quarry is reached, knee-deep snow also immobilizes the hunter. At javelin length, one misstep makes for a wasteful death under giant hooves. Skilled hunters were too valuable to sacrifice.

Many other places in the high plains offered Paleo-Indians good terrain for the hunt, but Sapello had everything: the sweet water of Sapello Creek, a little valley hidden behind the row of hills exposed to the plains, and a long outcropping ridge of flinty-gray andesite at the back of the valley—an important source of material for stone tools.

Lance heads of nearly every major Paleo-Indian era have been found nearby: Clovis, Folsom and Midland, Plainview, Cody, and Eden. For more than six thousand years flint-knappers painstakingly manufactured Sapello's sharp, gray stone into weapons of the hunt. The stone itself is remarkable—medium-gray, and easily worked when first exposed to light and air at the ancient diggings, it hardens gradually, becomes brittle, and soaks up the color of surrounding soil as it ages.

Sapello's tools have been found as far east as the Clayton-Clovis area and as far west as Grants. They have been found in sand dunes near Santa Rosa and as far south as the white sands of the Tularosa Basin, beyond Carrizozo. Near Belen, reddish clays transform the Sapello stone into a golden rust, while the Tularosa's white gypsum gives it a soft, chalky cast. Wherever these tools happen to be found, they were quarried from the little ridge of exposed stone at the edge of Sapello's hidden valley. There men rearmed for the hunts.

Sapello's heyday came during Eden times, about 6,000 B.C. By then, the giant bison were extinct, replaced by huge herds of smaller, almost modern, buffalo. Eden lanceheads were wicked spikes, five to six inches long, and flaked with great skill. Years ago, the Smithsonian Institution excavated an Eden site, called "R-6," near the crossroads. Archeologists recovered many broken Eden points in various stages of manufacture. Here, seven thousand years ago, a handful of the

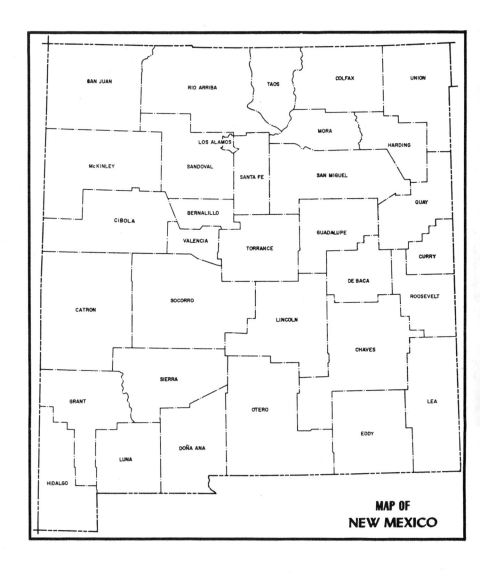

MAP OF
NEW MEXICO

Masonry walls exposed at an Anasazi pueblo. Photograph by
Rory P. Gauthier.

most skilled stone workers of their age had set up a small
"assembly line" to produce lanceheads.

Some Eden hunting sites were huge. A hundred buffalo or
more were skinned, butchered, and divided among the fortunate. Then small bands drifted away to camps in more
protected country. From one of these camps in Gallinas
Canyon, at Las Vegas's backdoor, can be seen the striking
roof-line of Montezuma's Castle.

Still others came to Sapello. Archaic hunters camped
there sporadically between 5,000 B.C. and A.D. 500, but
made tools of obsidian, so the little andesite quarry was forgotten. Even later, mounted Apache hunters came, sweeping
out of the plains to drive buffalo herds against New Mexico's
rocky backbone. Clusters of stone "tipi rings" are all that
remain of their huge fall buffalo camps. The fruits of these
provided for Apache families through three hundred bitter
winters on the high plains.

Right: Sapello: "...little tongues of grassland end in ponderosa-studded
coves...." Photograph by Cynthia M. Stuart.

18

Then came the "market" hunters. In the 1860s, the Civil War and railroad ventures drew a new breed of plainsmen. First armed with single-shot Sharps rifles, then heavy-caliber Winchester repeaters, men pursued buffalo across New Mexico's plains—for profit. Buffalo meat supplied forts, mining camps, and railroad gangs, while hides by the ton were shipped east to fascinated purchasers. In less than two decades, the great herds had vanished in an acrid cloud of black powder.

Now the Indian's great buffalo camps are gone. Only sky and grass and bubbling water remain. *Sah-PAY-o.* Say it out loud. *Sah-PAY-o.* Say it softly. Now whisper it—**Sah-PAY-o.* That is the sound made by the wind as it moans along the creek. It is God's own sigh, the breath of His sorrow, for after nearly seven hundred generations the buffalo no longer return.

*Note: Locally, Sapello is often pronounced *SAH-piyo.*

RECENT PALEO-INDIAN FINDS TELL NEW STORY

It was once thought that Paleo-Indian people, our state's first inhabitants, lived primarily on the eastern plains. Early finds of their tools were concentrated on the Llano Estacado, the flat, water-scarce grasslands that straddle the Texas-New Mexico border. It is now known that Paleo-Indian sites are scattered throughout New Mexico. More will undoubtedly be found in areas where previously no one expected to find them.

Although not the most ancient remains, the first Paleo-Indian site found in America was excavated in 1927 and named for the nearby village of Folsom. Folsom, thirty miles east of Raton, marks the western margin of Union County's high plains. The Folsom site was nothing less than the world's first scientific proof that man had inhabited the Americas thousands of years before the Christian era.

New Mexico's oldest C-14-dated Paleo-Indian sites belong to the Clovis Period, about 10,000 B.C. Clovis people hunted and scavenged Mastodon and other giant animals of the late

Ice Age. But the elephants and other large creatures disappeared rapidly and bison dominated the grasslands by Folsom times. At Folsom, bones of twenty-three huge, extinct bison were found with elegantly fashioned flint lance heads. The Folsom Period is C-14-dated to between 8,000 and 9,000 B.C. Since the first Folsom find, archeologists have generally searched for Paleo-Indian sites in regions which once supported herds of bison. From about 9,000 B.C. on, Paleo-Indians hunted bison above all other game on the high plains. In fact, they eventually became downright flagrant about it. The average bison "kill" site from Folsom times yields the bones of nineteen animals. But 3,000 years later, Cody Period sites yield an average of 126 animals! That is an impressive pile of meat.

As one walks along it is often impossible to see a few stone flakes or the broken tip of an ancient lance head. The average Paleo-Indian site is definitely not a tourist attraction. Even the remains from an impressive one might look positively lonely in a shoebox. But those enormous piles of bison meat eventually left big piles of bison bones.

Out in the scrubby arroyos and draws of the eastern plains there are no large Pueblo villages to divert one's attention. So the early archeologists looked for bleached bones eroding from the sandy soil. Where there were bison bones there were often Paleo-Indian tools. Each success built up the idea that bison hunting was just about all that these folks did for a living.

Later, archeologists sought Paleo-Indian sites in western New Mexico's pockets of grassland. Areas like the San Augustin Plains of Socorro and Catron counties once supported bison herds, so there was no particular surprise when a number of scattered Paleo-Indian sites were found there.

But until recently no one looked in the higher mesa country or piñon lands where deer and other upland game might have been pursued. Research published last year indicates the Cebolleta Mesa region in southern Valencia County was occasional home to upland hunting parties for four thousand years or more. Other hunting stations are scattered about west central New Mexico's foothills.

Archeologists in western New Mexico specialize in locating Anasazi and Mogollon villages. Most simply do not expect to find Paleo-Indian sites. Not even the most up-to-date text-

21

books mention that Paleo-Indian sites have been found in both Grant and Hidalgo counties.

In 1967, while seeking Classic Mimbres sites in Hidalgo County, archeologists came across Paleo-Indian remains above Cloverdale Creek. There, 298 stone fragments were recovered. About one-third of them had been used as tools. These included broken lance heads, spokeshaves, and scrapers. Statistical comparisons of Cloverdale lance head thickness and stem width suggest these may be of a type known as "Belen." Named after finds near the Rio Grande railroad town, these have never been dated by the carbon-14 method. An educated guess would place these at 7,500 to 8,000 B.C. The Cloverdale Valley is in an oak-piñon vegetation zone at 5,400 feet above sea level. No bison bones have been found, and the area is not a good candidate for plains-style hunting.

Grant County's single published Paleo-Indian site is known as "Burro Cienaga No. 9." There, thirty-seven locally produced stone fragments were found to the east of the springs. One unfinished lance point had been used as a knife and is similar to ones produced at the end of the Folsom Period. There were also flakes used as scrapers, but most were waste from tool manufacture. There are grasslands around Burro Cienaga, but no bison bones were found here, either.

Remains from both of southwestern New Mexico's Paleo-Indian sites would not fill a large coffee can. Yet, when considered with other recent finds, they tell an important story. Paleo-Indian peoples inhabited a wide area of western New Mexico. Here, small, mobile family bands pursued upland game and collected wild vegetal foods. Although no grand bison kills are likely to be found, future discoveries should tell us more about life in western New Mexico five hundred to six hundred generations ago.

Clovis and Folsom lanceheads. Drawing by Scott Andrae.

Before 1930 or 1931, practically no one believed that Indians had roamed New Mexico much before the Christian era. In spite of a few dissenters, most scholars believed that the New World had been populated by Asians migrating across the Bering Straits not more than three or four thousand years ago. That, at least, was the official position of the Smithsonian Institution until Jesse Figgins of the Denver Museum (then the Colorado Museum of Natural History) excavated near Folsom, New Mexico, and finally proved otherwise. But Figgins was not the first actor in this affair. It began one afternoon, late in August of 1908. The skies opened and, in a few hours, more than a year's average of rain fell on Johnson Mesa, which separates New Mexico from Colorado, east of Raton. Below, the usually dry wash of the Cimarron River heaved with surfeit and most of Folsom was swept away with a roar. Some days later, George McJunkin, the black foreman at the Crowfoot Ranch, was riding along Dead Horse Arroyo, upstream from the Cimarron.

Near the head of the arroyo, the flood waters had cut deeply. More than ten feet below the arroyo's rim, a pile of ancient bison bones lay exposed. They caught McJunkin's attention, for the bones were far more robust than those of modern bison. McJunkin, then aged fifty-two, had lived in west Texas and New Mexico during the era of the last great bison hunts, so he had seen the bones of contemporary bison often enough. But, more than that, he was an unusual man for his time. A skilled surveyor, McJunkin was also an amateur student of natural history, and his saddlebags were usually stuffed with books—literature, geography, biology, the classics.

So George McJunkin dismounted to inspect the pile of bones. Mixed among them he found chert flakes and several distinctive fluted lance points—later to become known as "Folsom Points." McJunkin was read in anthropology and fully understood the significance of his discovery, yet he was not able to attract the interest of professional scholars for many years to come. A decade later, he and Ivan Shoemaker, the ranch owner's son, excavated at the arroyo and exposed more bison bones and another fluted point. These he sent to the Denver Museum.

The following spring the Denver Museum sent H. J. Cook, paleontologist, to Dead Horse Arroyo. There McJunkin assisted him in test excavations. These were promising, but the Museum did not send out a full excavation team until Jesse Figgins came to Folsom in the summer of 1926. By then, George McJunkin, scholar, surveyor, and bachelor cowman, had died in a little room attached to the rear of the Folsom Hotel.

The first few attempts to retrieve undisturbed Folsom points in place with bison bones were botched. But late in the summer of 1927, Figgins' crews finally achieved their delicate goal and wired A. V. Kidder, the great field archeologist then working at Pecos Pueblo, to come with others and confirm the evidence. They did. George McJunkin did not live to read Figgins' article, "The Antiquity of Man in America," which came out in the fall 1927 issue of *Natural History*, but the hunt for early man in America was on.

During the thirties there were many new finds of materials left by ancient hunters-gatherers. By 1940, Frank H. H. Roberts, who had excavated the huge Lindenmeier Ranch Site of the Folsom period in northern Colorado, applied the term Paleo-Indian (ancient Indian) and it stuck. By then it was also known that Folsom was only one of several Paleo-Indian tool-making traditions in America. Eventually, tools of the "Clovis Horizon," named after finds near Clovis, New Mexico, proved to be even more ancient.

Today, there is still much that we do not know about the earliest inhabitants of New Mexico, or of America. We do not know anything certain about their language, beliefs, or family organization. We also know little of their technology except in stone and, to a lesser extent, in bone, for the soil eats away at hides and wood over the millennia.

Even now, archeologists have not arrived at a satisfactory answer about just when the very earliest Indian populations migrated across the low-lying bridge of rock and soil that once extended across the Bering Straits between Alaska and Russian Siberia. There are archeological sites widely scattered across the Americas which hint at a much earlier age. In most of these, stone tools are cruder than those of the Clovis Horizon, and bone and wood may have been the most important materials of manufacture. Most archeologists currently accept the idea that America was first populated between twenty

24

and thirty thousand years ago, but the evidence is either not solid, or not universally accepted for artifacts of any period much before twelve to fourteen thousand years ago.

Eventually, the earliest noncontroversial dates for human habitation in New Mexico will be pushed backward in time. In most areas of New Mexico sites of great age lie many feet below the surface, so the majority of very early sites are found in areas of substantial erosion. The plains of eastern New Mexico are quite worn down by the action of wind and rain, as are portions of the Rio Grande Valley between Bernalillo and Socorro. The flat grasslands, called the Plains of San Augustin, west of Socorro, also yield much surface evidence of Paleo-Indian habitation.

It was once thought that Paleo-Indians lived primarily in the eastern plains, but archeologists now know that such sites are scattered throughout New Mexico and more will undoubtedly be found as survey archeologists become accustomed to locating them in areas where once no one expected to find them. In just the last several years, a number of Paleo-Indian localities have been found on the Jicarilla Reservation of northwestern New Mexico. Others have been found in the Gallegos Wash region of the Navajo Reservation near Farmington, and an important concentration of Paleo-Indian hunting sites has been studied on the Acoma Reservation near Grants. A number of these finds lie at elevations of more than 7,000 feet—a forested zone not previously thought to be much used by the ancient hunters.

In all of the American Plains and Southwest, an area of about half-a-million square miles, only one hundred Paleo-Indian sites have been excavated in the last half-century— about two per year, on average. But only two dozen of these have yielded samples of bones or charcoal which were successfully dated by the carbon-14 technique.

Only three of those dated sites are in New Mexico, so much of what we know about Paleo-Indian chronology comes from excavation elsewhere. Most Paleo-Indian finds are actually scatters of artifacts found on old eroded soil surfaces. Even though most are singularly unimpressive to the average eye, the most precious undiscovered archeological treasures in the American Southwest are not additional huge, "lost" Pueblo ruins, but modest, intact deposits of Paleo-Indian materials where artifacts of the various types can be dated by laboratory testing procedures.

25

Paleo-Indian people lived and hunted in New Mexico for at least five thousand years, between 10,000 B.C. and 5,000 B.C. We may never know just when they first came, or why their tool-making traditions disappeared. But, in 1908, we knew virtually nothing of all this. So, George McJunkin changed the history of archeology—and, each year, students of archeology throughout the world read of the Folsom Site in lonely northeastern New Mexico.

FOLSOM HUNTERS: NERVE, SKILL, AND HIGH-TECH

New Mexico's first fling with high technology began with the remarkable Folsom lance head. Although these lances were first discovered between Raton and Clayton, bands of Folsom hunters also lived in the Rio Grande Valley more than ten thousand years ago.

In those days, summers were somewhat cooler and forests were more extensive than now. Herds of an immense, now extinct, bison roamed rich grasslands and small numbers of camel, sloth, and direwolf survived from the waning Ice Age. It took nerve, skill, and the right technology for hunters on foot to bring down such game.

Folsom lance heads are superbly made. About two inches in length, most have distinctive flutes, or grooves, gouged out of one or both sides. A thinner, unfluted variety, often found in the same sites, is known as the "Midland" point. When attached to the bone foreshaft of a six-foot lance and launched with a wooden spear thrower, both projectiles had remarkable penetrating power. Folsom hunters needed that power. Even in 9,000 B.C., good hunters were too important to a group's survival to risk death by falling under the enormous hooves of a wounded bison.

Although Folsom and Midland projectiles were contemporary, they were produced by quite different manufacturing techniques. The creation of a Folsom point required complex stoneworking skills and removal of the flutes was an extremely delicate step. One estimate suggests that about twenty-five percent of all Folsom points were broken in manufacture. Others were fractured either from striking animal bone or hitting hard earth and stone if the target were missed. Thus, the majority of Folsom points found by archeologists are broken or fragmented.

Very short Folsom points are often found. Some have simply been resharpened after normal usage. Others were carefully remanufactured after a portion of the tip had been snapped off by torsional forces during skinning and butchering. Badly broken ones were frequently converted into hide scrapers.

Although the related Midland projectiles were thinner, the delicate step of removing the flute was eliminated. Fewer of these seem to have been ruined during manufacture. Some archeologists believe that only the most skilled flintknappers created fluted Folsom points for exchange with their fellows.

In the Rio Abajo, lovely shades of pink or cream stone were often selected, and unfinished Folsom blanks were carried over wide distances. Near Belen or Los Lunas, an archeologist can find point fragments of Washington Pass Chert, carried from the Chuska Mountains north of Gallup. At other sites, Folsom tools are made of flint found only at outcrops along eastern New Mexico's Caprock.

About thirty Folsom sites and tool scatters have been identified in the Rio Abajo district between Bernalillo and Belen. Other finds of solitary lance tips have been made on Albuquerque's West Mesa, in the foothills near Tijeras Canyon, and near Manzano, an abandoned village on Kirtland Air Force Base overlooking Albuquerque's south side.

Paleo-Indian use of the Rio Grande Valley was most intense during the Folsom period. There are more Folsom sites than those of all other Paleo-Indian periods combined. Several different kinds of site have been found.

"Armament" sites yield evidence of Folsom point manufacture. Hunters camped at these to prepare lance points for the ensuing hunt. Many are on high points overlooking the Rio Grande Valley.

"Processing" sites contain stone tools with evidence of "working wear" on the edges. These are located near the shorelines of extinct ponds and lakes. Animal carcasses were apparently skinned and butchered near prime hunting areas.

"Base camps" are sites where Folsom families camped for a few days or weeks at a time. The widest variety of tools were found at these. Most are located near possible sources of fresh water.

Several Folsom sites have been excavated in the Albuquerque area. A Folsom deposit was unearthed at Sandia Cave, east of Bernalillo, in the spring of 1936. Another, the Rio Rancho site, was investigated by Jerry Dawson in 1966–67. The Albuquerque Archaeological Society also excavated there during the 1967 season.

The Rio Rancho site was a family camp, rather than a "kill" site, and it may be the only completely excavated Folsom one in North America. No animal remains were recovered, but several oval areas of compacted earth were found. These are generally accepted as the faint remains of shelter floors. Thirty-six Folsom points were recovered, along with scrapers for hide, wood, and bone-working, knives, and a number of gravers. Dawson's analysis of these tools suggests that three different hunting bands may have used the site. He believes that small groups hunted bison along the river and occasionally camped together.

Such sites provide evidence of New Mexico's first "high-tech" boom. After more than a thousand years, it faded with the disappearance of the giant buffalo species. But by today's standards that was no flash in the pan.

PEACH SPRINGS—NAVAJO NATION

Peach Springs—the mere thought of it excites me! My friend Frank Broilo discovered New Mexico's westernmost Paleo-Indian site there some years ago. After many conversations about his finds, we at last stole time to visit and search for artifacts late in the winter of 1976.

About midnight, tired after the long drive down Route 666 from Shiprock, Frank and I made camp near Tohatchi. By early morning, palisades of frost rimmed the mud at our camp's edge. Dawn broke over a low mesa to the east, and slender threads of sunlight sparkled among the icy crystals.

Dirt roads are firm this morning, but warmer afternoons will soon bog the Navajo Nation in a sea of impassable mud. Frank has already started his battered Dodge van. The hood is up and he is wiring a modified metal thermos to the truck's manifold. We will have hot tea in ten miles or so. Last night

An ancient chert quarry in northern New Mexico. Photograph
by Rory P. Gauthier.

we ate cold Dinty Moore stew and washed it down with
ginger brandy, hot from the manifold.

As the old Dodge bounces down the pipeline road toward
the highway, a little faster than is comfortable, Frank talks
animatedly about Paleo-Indian times. Until his fascination
with archeology brought him to the Southwest, he was a
school teacher. Detroit's school children must have been
sorry to see him go—this morning's lecture is exciting and
concise.

From roughly 10,000 to 5,000 B.C. small bands of these ancient hunters-gatherers wandered New Mexico, leaving behind their distinctive lance and dart points. Frank wrote his graduate thesis about Paleo-Indian tool-making while enrolled at Eastern New Mexico University in Portales. His find at Peach Springs was a personal triumph. There, most of the stone used in tool manufacture came from deposits at Washington Pass, nearly fifty miles away in the mountains northwest of Tohatchi.

A few miles north of Gallup, Frank leaves the highway and turns east on a rutted, dirt track. After several teeth-jarring miles we arrive.

To the right, the land slopes sharply downward to a wide arroyo. There erosion has exposed several hundred acres of an ancient clay surface. It is a miniature "badlands." Stark, lumpy, and windswept, small layers of stony soil jut upwards from ancient clay.

A hundred yards from the road a long reef of veined basalt rock protrudes from the slope. It lies in several elongated courses that follow the lip of the draw. Each course is lower than the one before it and separated by crevices several feet wide—like a gigantic stone washboard. Infrequent rains have washed Paleo-Indian artifacts into the crevices and trapped them there. The entire site covers an area of about 1,000 square feet—the size of a modest house.

Brightly colored stone chips, wastage from artifact manufacture, lie scattered about. We collect a surprising variety of these in a few minutes. From these bits of stone Frank separates a number that range from a very pale pink to dull yellow to the color of weak coffee. All of these were carried here from Washington Pass.

The chert nodules quarried at Washington Pass six thousand to ten thousand years ago yield a creamy, glassy stone, razor sharp when properly flaked. The thinnest pieces are partially translucent. Paleo-Indian toolmakers particularly sought the delicate pink variety to fashion into lance heads, so we intend to keep a sharp lookout for it as we search among the basalt troughs.

The hunt for artifacts begins in a crevice about two feet wide. At its bottom, soil and twigs are mixed with pebbles, broken rock, and many small stone chips. The work proceeds slowly. Pocket knives become "pokers" to dig out buried flakes.

Soon a knife tip exposes a large, pink, oval chip the size of a watch dial. From one end a series of small flakes have been removed to create a semi-circular edge. It is a "Folsom Period" hide scraper, about ten thousand years old.

Only an expert could distinguish this scraper from ones found at the original Folsom site east of Raton or from hundreds found along Blackwater Draw between Clovis and Portales. Folsom toolmaker's unique "quality control" was so consistent that the stone used in manufacture is often the best clue to a particular artifact's place of origin. That is why tracking down the color, grain, and sources of stone is so important to archeologists.

More tedious poking among thousands of bright chips turns up only several small lance head fragments. These are often impossible even for experts to identify accurately. Few people realize that the tip portions of lance or arrow heads are far more nearly alike than stem and base parts, which vary more in shape because methods of attachment to wooden shafts changed at various times.

Noon comes. Discouraged, we are about to give up. Suddenly Frank whoops! In his palm is prize enough for any textbook—an intact Folsom lancehead! It is an exquisite pale pink with little speckles of darker, rose-colored inclusions— about two and one-quarter inches long and grooved like a bayonet. Even the distinctive but fragile Folsom "eared tips" have survived at each corner of the indented base. Such a perfect Folsom lancehead is a rare and impressive find.

On hands and knees we search every square inch near Frank's find, but the stone crevice yields no other prize. Reluctantly we pack up, wiring a fresh thermos of tea to the old van. We have business in Gallup this afternoon. Our time has run out.

Note: This article was written as a memorial to Frank J. Broilo, the first director of the Office of Contract Archeology at the University of New Mexico. Frank died suddenly on February 3, 1979, not yet forty years of age. He was an excellent field archeologist, and this visit to his "special" discovery is one of my most vivid memories of days spent as his associate at U.N.M.

PART III

TWILIGHT OF "HUNTING" SOCIETY AND THE DAWN OF AGRICULTURE

Basketmaker cave and slab storage pits: an early agricultural site. Drawing by Scott Andrae.

Between 5,000 B.C. and the time of Christ, the average family's world shrank. Population grew, and previously vast hunting territories became crowded. Corn, beans, and squash came to the southwest from Mexico during later "Archaic" times. Eventually the first villages sprang up, but early harvests were small, and agricultural life was hard.

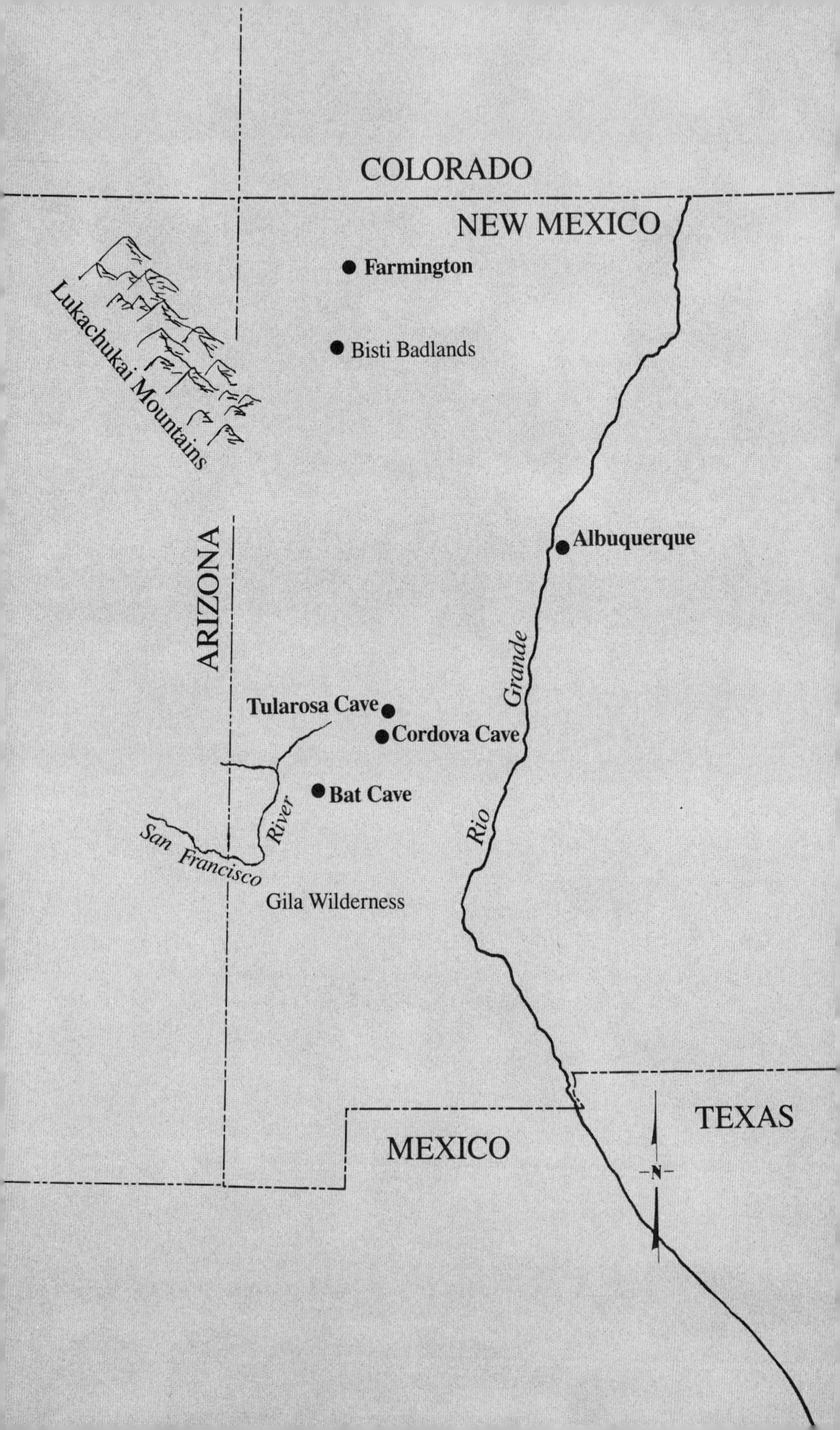
COLORADO
NEW MEXICO
Farmington
Bisti Badlands
Lukachukai Mountains
ARIZONA
Albuquerque
Rio Grande
Tularosa Cave
Cordova Cave
Bat Cave
San Francisco River
Gila Wilderness
MEXICO
TEXAS
N

Small family bands of Paleo-Indian hunters followed the buffalo and other game herds for nearly five thousand years. Homelands were vast, but people were few. Fall season hunting camps offered only rare opportunities to socialize, pick mates, and renew friendships. In time, climatic change reduced grasslands. Buffalo became scarcer, and classic hunting society was slowly transformed into an "Archaic" way of life. Starting about 5,000 B.C., an increasingly hotter, drier climate affected both the distribution and the kinds of plant and animal species. Early Archaic economy and technology resembled that of the late Paleo-Indian period. Since families stayed only a few weeks in one locale, each campsite represented only one stopping place on a ceaseless round of movement to seasonal food-producing areas. Later Archaic peoples hunted less often and the tendency towards family nomadism was severely restricted. A given family's world became smaller, more populated, and more precarious.

Archaic economic adaptation was unusually durable because a wide variety of plants and animals was exploited. In western New Mexico, the Archaic periods endured from about 6,000 B.C. to the birth of Christ, but lingered on in some areas of the eastern plains until A.D. 1000. Archaic peoples lived throughout New Mexico, and more than ten thousand sites of this period are known. Heavy concentrations of campsites and artifacts have been found northeast of Chaco Canyon, in the upper Pecos and Canadian river basins, and in the Rio Grande Valley. Archeologists find more Archaic sites in old sand dune "blow-outs" than in very mountainous settings. Most consist of only miscellaneous artifacts, flaked stone chips, and heat-cracked rock—produced by stone boiling techniques used in ancient cooking pits.

The early Archaic period is dated roughly to between 6,000 and 3,000 B.C. Development began earlier in southwestern New Mexico than in northern and eastern areas of the state. Farther west, in Arizona and California, an Archaic lifestyle was far more ancient.

Archaic economy differed from the Paleo-Indian in one basic respect. The food quest shifted to much greater emphasis on gathering wild plants and less on taking the largest

35

Jay point—last of the nomadic peoples' huge hunting lanceheads. Drawing by Scott Andrae.

game animals. Knives, scrapers, and other tools found with the earliest Archaic dart and lance points are more radically different from those of the Paleo-Indian period than are the points themselves, which were technologically similar for another thousand years.

In northwestern New Mexico the earliest Archaic lance head is called the *Jay* or "J," named after "J"[erry] Dawson who surveyed many of these sites in the 1960s. Some have been found as far south as Mescalero. Others, found in the Taos and Chama areas, are identical but have traditionally been called the "Rio Grande point."

Although Jay points resemble Paleo-Indian ones in some respects, seventy-five percent are made of glassy black basalt, a material seldom used by earlier peoples. The largest are formidable lance heads, four to five inches in length. Short ones were used on long, slender darts. Like earlier Paleo-Indian points, most have been ground smooth along the edges of the base. When attached to wooden shafts, smooth bases do not cut rawhide bindings.

Small Jay sites may be found in a variety of geographic settings, but the large base camps were generally located high in canyon heads, 6,500 to 7,000 feet above sea level. Jay period artifacts are often found mixed with Paleo-Indian tools in the same eroded surface sites. This suggests that upland hunting strategies were similar during both periods. Families returned regularly to the same base camps, and these often have ten or fifteen scooped-out earthen hearths filled with fire-fractured cobbles. Animal bones recovered there are usually those of rabbit, birds, fox, and deer, or antelope. Smaller Jay sites were typically in areas where specialized food-getting activities took place. Some were hunting stations. Others, primarily in old sand dunes, contain many chopping tools but lance heads are rare. At these places wild ricegrass, yucca, and other vegetal foods were collected. The "Bajada" period followed the Jay. Bajada sites are tentatively dated to the period between 4,000 and 3,000 B.C.—at the very height of the long hot period called the "Altithermal." In spite of this, Bajada population increased in the area northwest of Albuquerque, but there is no useful comparative information from other areas.

Unlike earlier periods, numerous cobble choppers, poorly made coarse scrapers, and cobble grinding stones are found. Evidently the peak of warm, dry conditions forced an even greater dependence upon plant foods, since well-made hide scrapers, previously common, are rare. An increased population, dry climate, and scarce food supply forced people to scrounge for every available food; grasses, roots, berries, nuts, seeds, rodents, and reptiles were undoubtedly eaten more often than large game.

These harsh conditions subdued classic hunting society for more than four thousand years until climate softened and tall grass drew new herds of buffalo to the eastern plains. There, often in the very shadow of ancient campsites, Apache and Ute hunters again came to trade, talk, love—and to skin buffalo—each fall.

A variety of Archaic Period lanceheads.
Drawing by Scott Andrae.

Waist deep in a test pit, John Beardsley grunts between each breath. His excavation lies about thirty feet from mine, near the ridge of the dune. The rhythmic pounding of his pick has not missed a beat in twenty minutes. Our portable radio blares the time and temperature. It is 108 degrees at the Farmington airport, 30 miles to the northwest of us. Here in the sand dunes it is even hotter. We have been excavating yard-square test pits for five days. Earlier, survey crews located a dense cluster of "Archaic Period" sites in these dunes. Most visible Archaic sites are hopelessly eroded scatters of stone flakes, charcoal, and heat-cracked rock from ancient cooking fires. They are often uncovered as wind creates depressions, or "blow-outs," in old sand dunes. Still, these finds raised hopes of uncovering intact cultural deposits that would tell us something about a poorly understood period in southwestern prehistory. We know the broad outline of Archaic events, but many details still elude us.

At roughly 3,000 B.C., a wave of change rippled over New Mexico, softening the agonizing technological conservatism which had gripped the state for nearly seven thousand years since Clovis times. Newcomers drifted in from the west, carrying a dart point known locally as "San Jose," elsewhere called "Pinto Basin."

After a long earlier period of harsh, dry climate, New Mexico became cooler and wetter during "San Jose" times. Population then expanded rapidly and family bands no longer enjoyed exclusive use of vast foraging territories as they had during the Paleo-Indian period. Thus, most of the diet came from wild plant foods while hunting was restricted. Eventually, family groups settled into ever more densely inhabited homelands and some began to cultivate corn and squash.

For decades archeologists have taught university students that the adoption of domesticated plants led immediately to an "agricultural revolution." This was based on the idea that the advantages of a secure food supply were so clear as to create rapid and stunning social development. But events in New Mexico simply do not support this dramatic view.

Here, the first stands of corn were only tended on a part-time basis and contributed little to the total diet. Over the course of more than one thousand years, from 1,800 B.C. to 500 B.C., garden plots did become more important, but no explosive changes took place. Our research team wants to understand why, and thus, with high hopes, we are digging here.

So far our work has been disappointing.

In the seventh test pit, my own, the first six inches consisted of sand, mixed randomly with artifacts from several Archaic periods. Below that lay a thin layer of reddish, sandy soil, stabilized by roots of the Indian rice grass which carpets the dune. That layer contained one nice "San Jose" dart point, a small scraper, several fractured cobbles, and a tiny shell bead.

"San Jose" points are stemmed and wickedly barbed. They date from about 3,000 B.C. to 1,800 B.C. The points are common but scarce in these dune sites, which were primarily places for processing collected plant foods. However, ornaments like the bone bead are very rare until much later in the Archaic period.

The pleasure of this find is short-lived. Moments later my trowel turns up the brass base of a .45–70 Winchester cartridge in the same level of sandy soil. Freeze, thaws, rain, wind, burrowing rodents, and the hooves of Navajo sheep all contrive continually to shift artifacts to different locations in this loose sand and soil. The shell bead appears to be *Olivella.* It might be two thousand years old or have been made at Santo Domingo Pueblo only twenty years ago and traded to a Navajo shepherd as "hishi"—still a well-known tourist commodity.

As the last of the reddish soil is cleared away in Pit No. 7, a hard-veined ancient surface is exposed. It is a dark gray clay—formed at the bottom of seasonal rain ponds long before this area of sand dunes was carved by great arroyos with names like Piñabete, Cottonwood, and Captain Tom's Wash. This soil layer is "sterile," containing no cultural deposits. My own hopes for a find are dashed.

It has been the same frustrating story at each test pit. One can continue to dig for a foot or a yard and turn up nothing more left by human hands. John Beardsley has dug more than eight feet into the heart of the dune. Before we take the disappointing news back to the University of New Mexico, he has decided to sink one test pit "to China" to make absolutely certain that no culture-bearing deposits lie below. He still hopes to find something in deeper, more ancient, and undisturbed soil.

Suddenly the rhythmic pounding stops! The silence is impressive. At three o'clock on a July afternoon these badlands simmer under a surrealistic hush, and every living thing holds its breath waiting for the cool embrace of sundown. Has John found another culture-bearing deposit? Unable to withstand the suspense, I yell, "John, what have you found?"

"Nothing. I can't believe it! Nothing! But I'm going to do this test pit by the book anyway. I don't ever want to hear a word about how we didn't go deep enough to find anything!"

Moments later, a tinny, scraping noise drifts down from John's pit. He has started to smooth or "face" its dirt walls with a hand trowel. Careful trowel-work yields a cross-section, or "profile," of the soil layers in the pit's wall. Each layer is then sketched and described for type of soil, texture, and color. These provide a permanent record of deposited layers, or stratigraphy.

Perspiration clouds my vision; tired and disappointed, I stop to change sweat bands and sip cool tea. The low, blue rim of the Lukachukai mountains, forty miles to the west, crackles in a salty haze. As my eyes absorb the barrenness of the Bisti Badlands, I too hold my breath and wait for sundown.

*BAT CAVE ONCE HELD RECORD
ON MOST ANCIENT CORN*

In June of 1948, a team of archeologists sponsored by Harvard's Peabody Museum was making scientific news at an unlikely spot in west-central New Mexico. Excavations at the mouth of Bat Cave yielded primitive, small-cobbed corn. This was later dated by the Carbon-14 method and for some years held the record as the oldest found in North America.

Bat Cave lies ten dusty miles south of Horse Springs in

Catron County. There, the southern margin of the San Augustin Plain ends abruptly and volcanic cliffs jut upwards. Today the surrounding landscape is dry and scrubby, but it was not always that way. The cave was carved from those cliffs by wave action of ancient Lake San Augustin. About twelve thousand years ago the extinct lake measured 11 miles by 34 miles and was more than 150 feet deep. Paleo-Indian lance heads of the Folsom Period have been found in the vicinity and indicate that hunters were drawn to the receding shoreline as early as ten thousand years ago. By 4,000 or 5,000 B.C. the lake was gone, victim of a major dry period.

Bat Cave was utilized by various Indian groups for at least five thousand years. From late Paleo-Indian times to about A.D. 1100, successive layers of debris were deposited. They provide a remarkable record of changing technology and economy.

The earliest inhabitants were hunters and vegetal collectors of the late Paleo-Indian Period. Several distinctive early dart points were recovered. One triangular point type, known as "Augustin," is found at a number of early sites in west-central New Mexico. Another, the "Bat Cave" point, has projecting "ears" at the stem's corners. Although scarce in New Mexico, these are similar to ancient lance points found at mountain hunting sites scattered through Central and South America.

The next occupants were the Archaic Period "Chiricahua" people. The earliest deposits of this period were variously dated at 2,000 to 4,000 B.C. It stunned archeologists to find primitive popcorn-like pod corn in these early levels. This had always been considered a period when small nomadic family bands collected seeds, grasses, and hunted primarily small game.

Prior to Bat Cave excavations, archeologists believed that both pottery manufacture and agriculture had arrived from Mexico about the time of Christ's birth. But here, corn predated pottery by nearly two thousand years. Suddenly outdated was a lot of scientific theory about how agriculture created rapid technological "revolutions."

Early Bat Cave agriculturalists apparently spent little time tending corn. For more than a thousand years the harvest was but one of several regular food getting activities. Small family

41

bands continued to travel, gather, and hunt through most of the year.

Squash was also grown at an early period. But the kidney bean did not appear in the cave until about 1,000 B.C. By that time, the widely found "San Pedro" dart points were predominant. Many kinds of bone and stone tools were manufactured. A surprising variety of objects were woven of hair, grass, or yucca fiber. These include well-made baskets, nets, and several types of sandals. The cob of San Pedro Period corn had increased in size, and it was comparatively plentiful. The presence of fragmentary wooden agricultural implements and numerous grinding stones indicates much more attention was placed on the fruits of harvest than in earlier times. Bison bones were also consistent finds during this late pre-pottery period.

Mogollon pottery appeared shortly after the birth of Christ and the technological accoutrements of settled village life eventually ended up as debris on Bat Cave's floor. Yet larger cobbed corn had become abundant in the cave's deposits by A.D. 1100. Then Mimbres Society faded and Bat Cave was forgotten for eight hundred years, its trove of ancient corn largely undisturbed. That proved fortunate for archeologists.

Few realize that when the Peabody Museum's investigators came to Catron County the exact age and origins of corn— one of Native America's greatest contributions to human society—was still the subject of obscure theorizing among scholars. Even fewer realize that archeologist Herbert W. Dick and his excavation crews did more than overcome the summer winds, mud, rainstorms, and mosquitos at Bat Cave. They helped set off one of science's greatest "Treasure Hunts"—the search for even earlier corn in the dry caves of northern and central Mexico.

Eventually, that treasure hunt led to discovery of the world's first corn, recovered during well-publicized excavations in the high, arid Tehuacan Valley of central Mexico. So today's archeologists know a great deal about the domestication of corn and its evolution from small to large cobbed modern varieties. Many have now forgotten that Bat Cave once played an exciting role in all of this.

GILA WILDERNESS—HOME OF NEW MEXICO'S
FIRST PREHISTORIC VILLAGES

The first snows have already fallen in southwestern New Mexico's vast, forested Gila Wilderness. A brilliant November sun warms resin-coated evergreens, adding pine scent to crystalline mountain air, while melted snow cascades to the ground. Thousands of people are drawn to this rugged sprawling country each year—most to enjoy the beauty and isolation of nature "unspoiled" by human endeavor. Few, however, realize that among these canyons, piñon groves, and clear, icy streams, New Mexico's first prehistoric villages were created. About sixteen hundred years ago, today's "wilderness" was the most densely inhabited region in the state.

It was around A.D. 250 when prehistoric Mogollon people began to consistently build small pithouse villages in the Ponderosa-fringed upland meadows of west-central New Mexico. Nearly half a century ago the Tularosa and Cordova cave sites were excavated in Catron County's Pine Lawn district. Although not genuine village sites, these dry caves yielded a well-preserved record of the transition to early agricultural villages. Dozens of textbooks commemorate these finds by designating the first Mogollon villages as the "Pine Lawn Phase." Over the years many pithouse sites have been found along the San Francisco River and adjacent forest areas. Here New Mexico's first pottery was made—a simple brown ware named after the contemporary village of Alma.

These villages typically consisted of five to twenty shallow, timber-roofed dugouts, or pithouses. House shape, depth, and size varied. Some were round, others squared, and many were shaped like a pinto bean. Some pithouses had central fire hearths, while others had none. Archeologists disagree on the meaning of specific variations but accept the idea that village life was still in an experimental stage. Even the basic economy varied from site to site and from one locale to another.

The famous "SU" site in the cool, Ponderosa-studded Pine Lawn region yielded remarkable numbers of stone *manos* and *metates*, essential corn-grinding implements. A good number of hunting implements and stone dartheads were also found

Manos and metates—essential corn-grinding implements. Photograph by Leonard Raab.

there. This indicates that hunting was an important supplement to small-scale agriculture. About a hundred miles to the southeast, the Harris site lies in the warmer, less wooded Mimbres Valley below Silver City. It yielded mainly agricultural implements, with little evidence of hunting. Another village site, Winn Canyon, overlooks the Gila River in Hidalgo County. There, pithouses contained mostly hunting implements but little evidence for agriculture.

Domesticated corn was brought to the area from Mexico between 1,500 and 2,000 B.C. but it did not have a rapid impact on daily life. This early corn was of a small-cobbed variety called *Chapalote*. Yields were low and for more than a thousand years small stands were tended only on an occasional basis.

For decades archeologists were troubled by the slow pace of change in New Mexico once corn had been introduced. It had long been assumed that the introduction of domesticated crops produced such an instant advantage that there should be a rapid "revolution" away from the old nomadic hunting-gathering economy. Partly because of excavation here in New Mexico, scholars now know that the change from nomadic hunting and gathering to agricultural villages proceeded very slowly in some cases.

It took field work among remnants of the world's nomadic peoples and in remote agricultural villages to discover the reasons. Under conditions of very low population density, nomadic hunter-gatherers earn a living with only 500 per capita hours of labor each year and malnutrition is surprisingly rare! Unsophisticated agriculturalists require more than 1,000 per capita hours annually to do the same, but malnutrition and infant death are more common. So are crop failures.

It turns out that early agriculture was both a lot of work and a gamble, given New Mexico's unpredictable weather. As long as prehistoric population was small, hunting and collecting provided an easier living, so settled village life was not an easy step. In New Mexico it was not taken until population had grown so that not everyone could hunt and collect wild plants, thereby guaranteeing a secure living. Even then not everyone settled into village life.

The first villages grew in scattered pockets. Although not all were lived in year-round, they were definitely home bases. Nomadic people the world over carefully avoid their dead. Not so the early Mogollon villagers, whose dead are buried among the pithouses.

Within several centuries, small villages spread to other parts of western New Mexico—to the El Paso area, Albuquerque's West Mesa, and to far northern locations. Mogollon villages continued to flourish in the Gila country until roughly A.D. 900, when entire clans moved into the surrounding lowlands. In the early A.D. 1200s, when the Gila cliff dwellings were built, drought forced many to return, but times were hard and the cool forests and deep canyons were permanently abandoned by A.D. 1350. It now surprises many to discover that Acoma and Taos Pueblos have been lived in longer than the Gila has been true wilderness.

PART IV

CHACO AND MIMBRES: HEYDAY OF THE ANCIENT SOUTHWEST

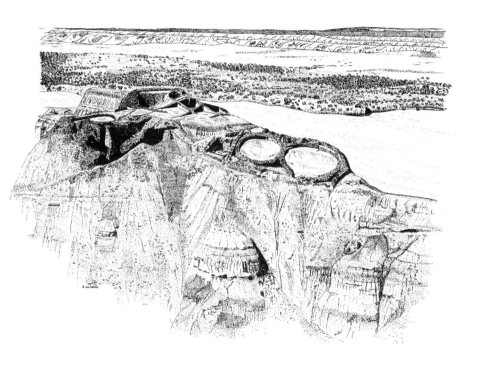

Bis' sáni Ruin, A.D. 1130s. Probably the last Chacoan stronghold ever built. Drawing by Scott Andrae.

Between A.D. 250 and 900 both Anasazi and Mogollon farmers gradually developed pithouse villages and stabilized agricultural techniques. Then, about A.D. 950, southwestern society exploded in an orgy of growth. More than 10,000 pueblo-style villages were founded in only 150 years between A.D. 950 and 1100! While the Anasazi built great roadways and huge sandstone citadels, Mimbres pottery was traded over an area of 40,000 square miles.

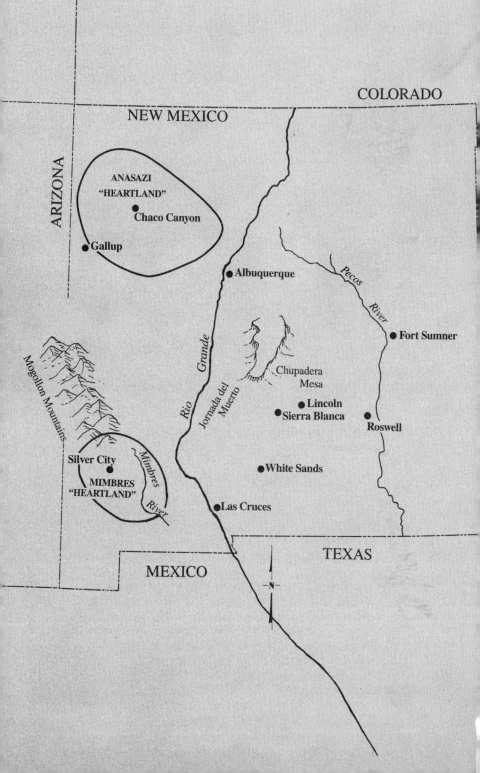

PART IV

CHACO AND MIMBRES:
HEYDAY OF THE ANCIENT SOUTHWEST

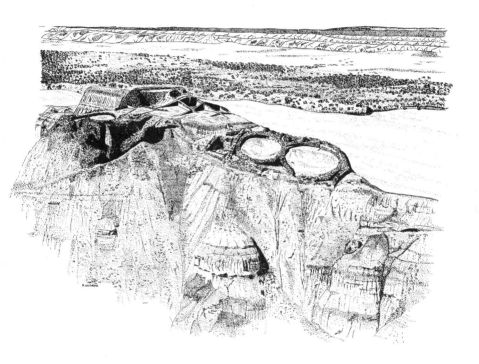

*Bis' sáni Ruin, A.D. 1130s. Probably the last Chacoan stronghold ever built.
Drawing by Scott Andrae.*

*Between A.D. 250 and 900 both Anasazi and Mogollon
farmers gradually developed pithouse villages and stabilized
agricultural techniques. Then, about A.D. 950, southwestern society exploded in an orgy of growth. More than
10,000 pueblo-style villages were founded in only 150 years
between A.D. 950 and 1100! While the Anasazi built great
roadways and huge sandstone citadels, Mimbres pottery was
traded over an area of 40,000 square miles.*

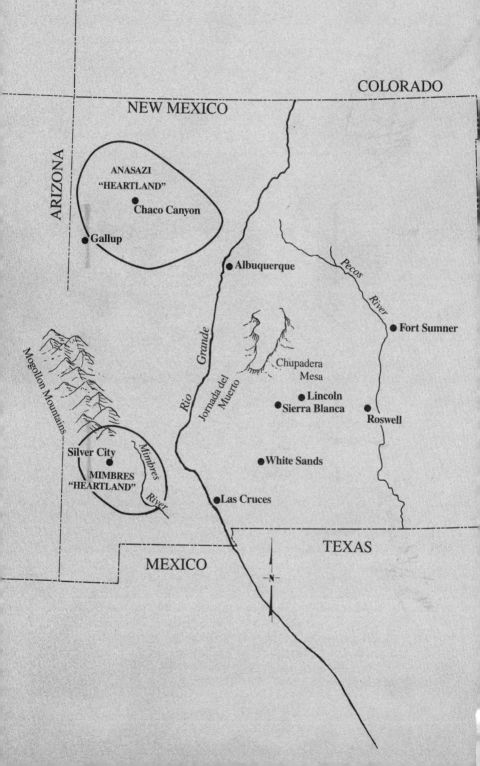

COLORADO

NEW MEXICO

ARIZONA

ANASAZI
"HEARTLAND"

● Chaco Canyon

● Gallup

● Albuquerque

Pecos River

● Fort Sumner

Rio Grande

Jornada del Muerto

Chupadera Mesa

● Lincoln
● Sierra Blanca

● Roswell

Mogollon Mountains

Silver City
●
MIMBRES
"HEARTLAND"

Mimbres River

● White Sands

● Las Cruces

MEXICO

TEXAS

N

*Whirlwind House . . . . Muddy Water . . . . Bee Burrow Ruin
. . . . Coyote Sings Here.* These names are more than poetry;
they are part of the most remarkable array of archeological
ruins in all of North America. In prehistoric times, a great
network of roadways radiated outwards from Chaco Canyon
National Monument. These once connected impressive sandstone citadels and large pueblo villages into a political and
economic network worthy of the grandest feudal baron.
Archeologists refer to this as the "Chaco Phenomenon," and
it has received lavish publicity. For all that, few people realize just how vibrant, how brief, and how fragile was the
world created by Chaco Anasazi farming peoples a millennium ago.

The Chaco Anasazi once inhabited the northwestern
quarter of New Mexico and adjacent areas of Arizona, Utah,
and Colorado. Their territory included nearly 40,000 square
miles, an area larger than Scotland. It has taken archeologists
fifty years of tedious survey on foot to locate more than ten
thousand Anasazi ruins. These were created in the nine hundred years between A.D. 400 and 1300. But a stunning forty-
three percent, or 5,000 of these ruins were built in only 150
years, between A.D. 950 and 1100! This powerful surge in
village construction marks the heyday of the Chaco Anasazi.
Everyone agrees that the roadworks were developed at some
time during this period.

Most of the Anasazi ruins are small, scattered masonry-
based pueblos of six to twenty rooms. Average ones have a
floor area of from several hundred to several thousand
square feet. These dot the basinlands and mesas of San Juan,
McKinley, and Cibola counties. Areas of especially good soil
and dependable water eventually drew more impressive concentrations of farmsteads. A number of these, like the settlement known as *Kin Ya'a*, grew into extensive farming centers, with dozens of free-standing pueblos, or roomblocks,
scattered over a square mile or so.

Archeologists have never been surprised to find large,
distinctive masonry buildings erected at many of the farming
centers. These "Great Houses," often multistoried, vary in
size, but most are massive sandstone strongholds enclosing

49

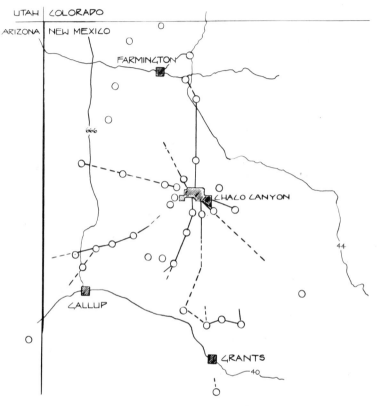

UTAH | COLORADO
ARIZONA | NEW MEXICO
FARMINGTON
666
CHACO CANYON
44
GALLUP
GRANTS
40

KNOWN CHACO ROADS

○ PREHISTORIC STRUCTURES

N   0   10   20 MILES   JOHN R STEIN

circular ceremonial chambers, or kivas. The number of kivas may be few or many, but two are commonly found enclosed in rectangular, monolithic cells of outsized rooms. These rooms are often without cooking hearths and artifacts. Some appear to have been purposely kept free of debris and clutter. Archeologists disagree whether these were used as granaries, barracks, or the private apartments of local elites in Chacoan society.

Other "Great Houses" were built in unlikely places—smack in the middle of nowhere. The farming centers that should have grown to require public facilities just were not there. One example, the huge rectangular citadel or *Pueblo Pintado*, lies on Chaco's isolated eastern frontier, about twenty miles from the major towns in Chaco Canyon. It once stood at least three stories tall, and sixty immense ground floor rooms enclosed seven kivas. Yet tree-ring dates suggest it was constructed rapidly in A.D. 1060 or 1061.

We now know that a prehistoric roadway connected *Pueblo Pintado* to the large towns in Chaco Canyon. From the ground, no roadway can be seen today, only a faint line of sagebrush runs into the distance. But airplanes have a better view.

Like the road to *Pintado*, most of the several hundred miles of suspected prehistoric roadways were first located on aerial photographs. "Remote sensing" specialists in Albuquerque began to identify possible roads a few years ago. They quickly learned that, when photographed in midday sun, the roads were usually invisible, while aerial photographs taken in the oblique rays of early morning sunlight made the ancient linear roadways stand out.

Several years ago a team of government archeologists decided to find out which of the "roads" identified on aerial photographs were real and just how old they were. This immense job continues, but initial results have been exciting. Segments of suspected roadway were surveyed on foot, test-trenched, and analyzed geologically. Some "roads" turned out to be fence rows. Others were recent. The team's geologist showed that the pressure of wagon and auto wheels on historic roadbeds compacted underlying mud into distinctive semi-circular soil plates. Though easily visible, no compression plates were found in trenches which crosscut roads connecting a number of ruined Anasazi towns. These were the real thing.

The Chaco roads were originally ten to thirty feet wide and had raised shoulders. Uniformity was important. Some sections were excavated, or graded, while others were built up. Their earthen surfaces were cleaned regularly and repaired when damaged by floods or erosion.

Today, in only a few places do the prehistoric roads still look like a road, so aerial photographs guided the archeological survey crews. By following these, previously unknown ruins were found. Some were "Great Houses;" others were new and puzzling. Several dozen small, semi-circular stone walls were located on high vantage points along roads. Called "herraduras," or horseshoes, these often marked places where two roads diverged. They may have been windbreaks or stopping places.

Most Chacoan roads ran straight and did not curve with the terrain. Stone steps were cut into unavoidable cliff faces and detours often were marked by double grooves chiseled in bedrock. Some road segments were dual, like divided highways. In places these were also marked by stone grooves. To date, the great "North" and "South" roads from Chaco Canyon are best known. The former runs north fifty miles to Salmon Ruin near Bloomfield. The other runs south to the Chacoan towns between Grants and Gallup, passing through *Kin Ya'a.*

Archeologists currently believe more than eighty Anasazi towns were connected to Chaco Canyon by roadways. One of the oldest farming districts was in the Red Mesa Valley between Grants and Gallup. Later, new towns were built and roadways were extended north to Colorado. In Chaco's final hour, sites like Aztec Ruin were built on the northern frontier. They generally date to the early A.D. 1100s.

It will take years to investigate the first road system in the United States, and archeologists may never master all the details necessary to completely explain the Chacoan period. We do not even know with certainty which languages were spoken, nor how many tribal groups were involved in Chacoan development. But the basics of what actually happened are reasonably clear.

During the late A.D. 800s and early A.D. 900s population expanded rapidly. The number of villages and farmsteads increased dramatically. Economy shifted from mixed agriculture and upland hunting to increased dependence on the dry-farming of large-cobbed varieties of corn. Rainfall was not greater than today, but most came in late summer and was stable from year to year during much of the period. Efficient agricultural practices and extensive economic networks tapped the full potential of this climatologic consistency. There was a frenzy of building activity, art, politics, religion, and trade flourished.

The transition to the Chacoan period first took place in the lower, drier elevations of northwestern New Mexico. Early sites are characterized primarily by small roomblocks of above-ground masonry architecture, metates with more grinding surface, and the introduction of pottery types such as Red Mesa Black-on-white. The pre-Chaco style of pithouse village quickly faded from the scene.

During the Chacoan expansion there were several major shifts in settlement patterns. The first of these, about A.D. 900, involved a brief upstream move in village location. This relocation was dramatic in the Navajo Reservoir district and in the Chuska Valley north of Gallup. By about A.D. 950 this initial upstream/uphill movement terminated, and the essential settlement characteristic of the Chaco Anasazi emerged. At this time there was a major downhill shift in village locations. Well-forested areas were abandoned, and there was increasing dispersal of small pueblos and farmsteads throughout the western basins. This expansion eventually spilled out of the San Juan Basin.

By about A.D. 1050, the dispersal of pueblo style farming villages was near its maximum, reaching to the upper Pecos River valley. Continued settlement in forested, highland areas is notoriously hard to document during the heyday of the Chaco Anasazi, yet many archeologists have been slow to accept this. In the Gallina highlands between Navajo Reservoir and Cuba there was a general abandonment of upland villages between A.D. 950 and 1100. Population in the cool, forested Mesa Verde region was lowest during the late Chacoan period, and the Zuni Mountains southwest of Grants were largely vacated from roughly A.D. 1000 to A.D. 1200.

Economic patterns clearly illustrate the major shifts in settlement during the Chacoan period. During the initial transition, trade in ceramic materials and in exotic goods of many kinds increased dramatically over a wide geographic front. First, diverse ceramic styles developed rapidly in areas

Window detail at Chetro Ketl, Chaco Canyon, 1920. Photograph by Wesley Bradfield. (Neg. no. 80517, courtesy Museum of New Mexico.)

Pueblo Bonito at Chaco Canyon. (Neg. no. 68810, courtesy Museum of New Mexico.)

Black-on-white Anasazi jar, found near Pueblo Bonito, Chaco Canyon. Photograph by Arthur Taylor. (Neg. no. 87196, courtesy Museum of New Mexico.)

bordering the upland perimeters of the San Juan Basin. This was followed by a rapid extension of economic networks into the central basin. By A.D. 1000, the middle of the Chacoan period, major adjustments in trading patterns had begun to take place. The frequency of ceramics traded into Chaco Canyon from the Red Mesa and Chuska Valleys changed over the course of time. By A.D. 1100, late in the period, production centers for ceramics had again changed, and economic activity focused on the Basin's northwestern margin and the southern approaches to Mesa Verde.

Few people realize that only a moderate percentage of the ceramics used at Chaco Canyon between A.D. 900 and 1150 were made there. Throughout, imports came from production centers at the periphery of the San Juan Basin. However, there was virtually no trade along the northeastern frontier, a "no man's land" which separated Chaco country from the Gallinas highlands in the area of present day Highway 44.

The food economy of the Chaco Anasazi period strongly depended on harvesting relatively large-cobbed corn and hunting very small animals. This latter pattern is striking. Most meat consisted of cottontail, jackrabbit, rodents, and small bird species. Domesticated turkey and wild vegetal foods supplemented garden crops. While some large game animals were taken, this use of small species is a hallmark of most Chacoan period diets.

There was substantial contact between the Chaco Anasazi of the San Juan Basin and villagers of the Quemado and Reserve districts to the south. Field research now in progress indicates that Chacoan roadways and villages may have penetrated as far south as Highway 60. The Gallup and Zuni areas seem to have been both important economic nodes and continuous sources of interchange from at least sometime in the A.D. 800s onward.

By about A.D. 1100, there had already been substantial Anasazi village expansion into the Galisteo Basin southeast of Santa Fe and eastward from the east slope of the Sangre de Cristos to the Las Vegas area. Here, there were no roadways and Chacoan influence was more tenuous. On the eastern periphery of the Anasazi homeland, villages were generally smaller, jewelry and tradegoods fewer, and harvests more modest. Settled village life only lasted several centuries in the hinterlands east of the Pecos River valley and was never re-established there until recent times.

By A.D. 1100 an enormous, complex, and extremely fragile, regional Anasazi system was sustained as the Chacoan network assumed its final form. Although the economic and demographic network which underlay this development began to emerge at important agricultural localities as early as A.D. 900, many of the "Great Houses" and public facilities were constructed between A.D. 1080 and 1120, at the very end of the Chacoan era. Perhaps this terminal complexity was in part induced by an already overstressed agricultural system. Excavation at late Chacoan sites has yielded ample evidence that infant mortality was shockingly high, malnutrition common, and early death the norm.

The Chacoan boom ended rapidly. In many districts, the abandonment of basin farmsteads began about A.D. 1100. By A.D. 1150, settlement and daily economy had shifted over nearly all of northwestern New Mexico. Although a few large Chacoan towns may have lingered on, isolated and in a depressed state, for another generation or two, most of the San Juan Basin was vacant. Some groups resettled near long abandoned villages in surrounding uplands, while others pioneered in forested districts north of Santa Fe. The Chaco Anasazi pattern of dry-farming large-cobbed corn and storing surplus for trade also ended. By the early A.D. 1300s, after more difficult times, irrigation agriculture replaced dry farming among Puebloan successors to the Chaco Anasazi.

Archeologists do not agree on the causes of Chacoan decline. Rainfall did become unstable in the early A.D. 1100s. Yet few societies fail because only one thing goes wrong. Perhaps one day we will know just which factors drove so vital a society to the twilight of the ambiguous, half-remembered legends passed down to today's Pueblo peoples. But for a time, roadways, granaries, and district trading villages wove nearly 40,000 square miles of scrubby basinlands into prehistoric North America's most remarkable economic and cultural force.

Following page: Ruins of Pueblo Bonito at Chaco Canyon. (Neg. no. 58339, courtesy Museum of New Mexico.)

THE BEGINNINGS OF MIMBRES ARCHEOLOGY:
SILVER CITY TAKES ON
THE EASTERN ACADEMIC ESTABLISHMENT

The period following New Mexico's statehood in 1912 was an exciting one for southwestern archeology. The great Anasazi ruins of northern New Mexico and adjacent regions had inflamed the public's imagination. In the East, three centuries of change had destroyed or obscured much of a pre-Columbian America, but here in the Anasazi country immense, rust-colored stoneworks still jutted upward into a turquoise sky. The National Geographic Society was intoxicated with Pueblo Bonito at Chaco Canyon. Many ruins at Mesa Verde had already been stripped of spectacular artifact troves in an earlier tangle of academic and not-so-academic excavation campaigns. This time, no one wanted to be left out.

Prominent Eastern universities, foundations, and museums competed with one another—and with local interests. Academic patricians, local ranchers, and district bureaucrats were sometimes thrown together in unlikely, even clandestine, drawing-room vignettes. It was a free-for-all! To victors went the excavation rights to entire Anasazi districts lying north of the Santa Fe rail line. No one paid much attention to smaller ruins in southern New Mexico's Gila and Mimbres river country. That is, almost no one.

Between 1910 and 1914, E. D. Osborn of Deming amassed a spectacular collection of "Mimbres" pottery bowls. These he sold to the National Museum (now part of the Smithsonian) for a handsome price. That set off an unglorious epoch of pot-hunting in Grant and Luna counties. The Mogollon people had not yet even been identified in textbooks, and much of what they had created was in danger from random looting.

Into this scene stepped Cornelius B. and Harriet S. Cosgrove of Silver City. The Cosgroves were not only prominent in local business and public affairs, but they were also anxious to protect and analyze the area's ruins. Between 1919 and 1923, they excavated their own Mimbres village at "Treasure Hill," published the results in *El Palacio*, and "jawboned" many ranchers into closing their ruins to haphazard

pot-hunting.

Eager for Mimbres archeology to prosper, the Cosgroves also negotiated research arrangements between local ranchers and universities, among them the Museum of New Mexico, the Southwest Museum, Beloit College, and the University of Colorado. Not content to stand on the sidelines, they took time to study excavation technique with the greatest field archeologists of the day: Alfred V. Kidder, excavator of Pecos Pueblo; Frederick W. Hodge, excavator of Hawikuh; and Neil M. Judd, excavator of Pueblo Bonito.

In 1924, the Cosgroves associated with the staff of Harvard's Peabody Museum. That year they took up the project that was to earn them immortality in the literature of archeology. The excavation of Swarts Ranch Ruin, not far from the junction of Highways 90 and 61 in the Mimbres Valley, required four seasons' work. The Cosgroves' son, Col. C. B. Cosgrove, Jr., now living in Albuquerque, assisted in the 1925 excavation campaign.

At Swarts Ruin, 172 rooms were excavated. Forty-seven of these were early pit-dwellings found underneath the aboveground houseblocks of the Classic Period. Some unplastered dug-out houses, although built in the A.D. 900s, contained "Boldface" Mimbres pottery. Techniques of pottery manufacture advanced more rapidly than architecture in Mimbres Country, and Boldface bowls were already nearly as refined as the later Classic Mimbres ceramics.

The overlying Classic Period houseblocks are dated between A.D. 1000 and 1150. These contained 125 rooms, well laid out in "north" and "south" house clusters. Village life focused on the central plaza, just as it does today in the Rio Grande Pueblos.

The village's occupants raised small-cobbed corn and collected wild foods such as yucca, grass seeds, and piñon nuts. No "pinto" beans or squash seeds were found in the ruin, but these may have rotted away.

An array of wild animals were eaten. These included deer, antelope, and buffalo, but rabbit, birds, and various rodents were more common. Large game had become scarce by late Classic times.

The Cosgroves retrieved many kinds of material goods and tools; manos and metates for grinding corn, shell beads, carved stone pendants, finger and ear rings, turquoise, and numerous arrow heads. However, the most remarkable aspect

Circular masonry kiva—typical of the Anasazi. Photograph by
Leonard Raab.

of the ruin lay under its hard-packed floors. Mimbres folk
literally buried their dead underfoot. From beneath the village's 172 rooms came 1,009 burials! Several rooms contained more than two dozen burials. Most had offerings of
beautiful black-on-white Mimbres bowls, and 635 of these
were found.

In 1932, Harvard's Peabody Museum published Cosgroves'
report, "The Swarts Ruin." The report has aged gracefully
into a venerable "classic"—a half-century later it was still
cited in the Smithsonian Institution's prestigious *Handbook
of North American Indians*. So, as the Ivy League scholars
manuevered for Anasazi digging rights, "Bert" and "Hattie"
Cosgrove of Silver City brought academic archeology to the
Mimbres country. Score two points for New Mexico.

Pioneer anthropologist Adolph Bandelier first systematically recorded a number of New Mexico's prehistoric ruins in the early 1880s. In the following half-century, archeologists were obsessed with the large Anasazi ruins in northwestern New Mexico. There they excavated and compiled data to identify major stages in southwestern prehistory. In 1927, results were codified into a chronology which came to be called the "Pecos Classification"—still used to this day. At that time the Anasazi world was considered to be the major source of southwestern development. Peripheral regions were typically treated as "rural" or "rustic" versions of Anasazi society. But the Anasazi sequence did not really match what the few field archeologists working south of Route 60 had begun to observe.

In the 1930s, several younger archeologists intensified research in southern New Mexico and eastern Arizona. One of the most daring, Emil Haury, published "The Mogollon Culture of Southwestern New Mexico" in 1936. "Mogollon" ruins were named after the Mogollon mountains in which most of the early finds were made. (The Mogollons extend westward into Arizona and were originally named after Don Juan Ignacio Flores Mogollon, provincial governor of New Mexico from 1712 to 1715.) Haury's "Mogollon Culture Areas" described a distinct archeological region and resolved problems with the Pecos sequence. The Mogollon chronology, like the Anasazi one, is divided into half a dozen periods. Pottery appeared a bit earlier among the Mogollon than among the Anasazi, but the Anasazi developed the "pueblo" style of architecture first.

In southern New Mexico Haury and others found archeological sites characterized by pithouses and, later, after A.D. 1000, by cobble and adobe "pueblos." Mogollon religious chambers were usually square, unlike those of the Anasazi, which are round. Everyday ceramics were brownwares rather than the graywares so characteristic of northern New Mexico's Anasazi country. Mogollon decorated ceramics were reds or red-on-browns until about A.D. 900. Thereafter, Anasazi color schemes penetrated the southern highlands. The Mogollon brown pottery is produced in an oxygen rich atmosphere, while the grays of the Anasazi are oxygen starved, indicating two different manufacturing techniques. Different types of pottery clay also contributed to regional characteristics.

Mogollon populations extended from, roughly, Socorro and south into northern Mexico. The heartland was in the area of the Gila Wilderness and extended westward into Arizona. The eastern periphery of the "pure" Mogollon district is west of the Rio Grande. But scholars argue endlessly about the exact location of the boundaries.

In the Mogollon area attention has been devoted largely to the so-called Mimbres people—named after the Mimbres River, which runs south from the Gila Wilderness to vanish in the desert near Deming. Mimbres means "willow trees" in Spanish. The area's early Spanish inhabitants first applied the name "Mimbreños" to pithouse villages along the river, since clumps of willow trees grew in the disturbed pithouse soil.

Presently, archeologists apply the term only to sites containing the distinctive Mimbres Black-on-white pottery and puddled adobe-cobble architecture—not to the pithouse villages. Mimbres villages represent the Classic period of Mogollon development from about A.D. 1000 to 1150. They are contemporaneous with Classic Chaco Canyon pueblos three hundred miles to the north, but are not so large, so numerous, or so architecturally refined. The famous Mimbres Black-on-white pottery, however, is elegant by any standard.

The Mogollon heartland was abandoned by roughly A.D. 1450. No living descendants can be conclusively identified.

To the east, the "Jornada-Mogollon Culture Area" was first defined by Donald Lehmer in 1948. The culture area is named for the Jornada del Muerto—the waterless region in Socorro and Sierra counties referred to as the "journey of the dead man" in accounts of Spanish expeditions. In reality, the Jornada del Muerto is but a small portion of the culture area. It has been expanded eastward since then. Now it encompasses most of southern New Mexico save the westernmost portion.

Here life-style was basically "Mogollon," but the pace of development was retarded. Sites are smaller, fewer in number, and prior to A.D. 800 villages are quite scarce. The farmsteads and other Mogollon characteristics diminish as one moves east toward the Pecos River. Somewhere in that area

Mogollon and Plains archeological features blend. So again, no precise boundary is agreed upon. In the Pecos region, agriculture and settled village life appear to have been prominent features for only a few centuries at the end of the first millennium A.D. Research there is still in its infancy and there are few dated ruins.

Hundreds of sites throughout the "Jornada" contain only ubiquitous brown utility wares, manufactured for nearly a thousand years, so one can only guess at a date. Much of the Jornada-Mogollon area was abandoned in the A.D. 1400s, then later resettled by Apachean groups. The core area, roughly bounded by Socorro, Carrizozo, Alamogordo, and Las Cruces, remains one of the least known archeological frontiers in North America. Some young archeologist will yet become famous unlocking secrets buried in the "Jornada frontier."

CLASSIC MIMBRES POTTERY
IS FOUND IN SURPRISING PLACES

I stood near the western boundary of White Sands National Monument and goggled at the pottery fragment in my hand. This sherd had come from the rim of a Classic period Mimbres bowl. The curved interior surface was finished a smooth cream. Two even lines the color of black coffee encircled the inside rim. Dozens more like it were scattered about. Mark Wimberly grinned over my shoulder. He and his partner, Pete Eidenbach, had brought me here from Tularosa, headquarters of their archeological foundation.

I had not expected to find this quantity of Mimbres pottery in the sandy scrublands of White Sands Missile Range. From where I stood it was about a hundred miles due west to the Mimbres country and its piñon-studded uplands. The sherd I held was virtually indistinguishable from ones found within ten miles of Silver City. To account for this, one had first to consider events in the Mimbres Valley.

About A.D. 900 pithouse villages in the Mimbres heartland began to bulge with expanding population. Eventually, new villages were founded in less favored locations along smaller creeks and washes. Local Mogollon society experimented with new technology. Pottery changed rapidly from traditional red and creams to classic Mimbres black-on-white

65

Mimbres bowl—black-on-black interior design. Photograph by Arthur Taylor. (Neg. no. 100686, courtesy Museum of New Mexico.)

designs. One intermediate pottery, carrying coarser black-on-white painted designs, is called "Boldface" and dated to A.D. 950 or 1000.

Mogollon society continued to grow until it erupted from the uplands of the Mimbres and Gila drainages, and a wave of population swept south and east. Dozens of villages containing Boldface pottery were founded in the sandy lowlands of Luna and Sierra counties between Deming and the Rio Grande. These farmsteads usually contain only several shallow pithouses. A number also have been found along the river between Truth or Consequences and El Paso, and "Boldface" pithouses have been excavated near Hatch, in Las Cruces's Mesilla Valley, and in El Paso. Small game, rodents, wild vegetal foods, and farming all contributed to the diet. Pithouses were seldom inhabited for more than a few years, and life was meager on the eastern Mogollon frontier.

Meanwhile, rapid change continued in the Mimbres homeland. Fully classic pottery was produced there by the first decades of the eleventh century—*before* the first pueblo style villages. By A.D. 1050, the large cobbled-adobe villages of the classic period were being constructed. These and the delicate black-on-white pottery formally identify the Classic Mimbres Phase of Mogollon society.

Along the Mimbres River, Classic village size averaged twenty rooms, but some eventually grew to two hundred rooms. In outlying areas like the Gila River villages averaged only nine rooms, and none grew to exceed one hundred. Farming was the primary occupation.

Shortly after development of the refined pottery, a second wave of population rippled eastward across the Deming Plain and the first cobbled-adobe villages were founded in the lowlands. This time, population and Classic Mimbres pottery penetrated the Jornada country across the Rio Grande and swept into the Tularosa Basin.

Throughout the Classic period, Mimbres black-on-white bowls were traded across southern New Mexico. Bits and pieces of these are found at ruins along the western foothills of the Sierra Blanca and Sacramento ranges from Carrizozo to Alamogordo. Most of these ruins are of modest size. Some are the remains of several pithouses, while a very few are cobble-adobe pueblos reminiscent of smaller villages in the Mimbres area. Occasional trade between the Silver City and

67

White Sands regions could account for the modest amounts of Mimbres pottery at these sites and the terracotta pottery from the Tularosa Basin which is found in the Mimbres Valley.

Sites that may have been Mimbres outposts are found sprinkled across the basin floors of Sierra, Otero, and Doña Ana counties. Unlike the foothill ruins, these are harder to explain. At some, acres of pottery sherds and fragmented stone tools litter the sandy soil. But most are puzzling. At these, there are no clear-cut architectural remains from houseblocks, plazas, and cooking hearths, so no tree-ring or carbon samples can be taken and dated. Some may have been constructed of puddled adobe, now washed away. Ones east of the Rio Grande are often found in sandy, barren areas that were unlikely farmlands. Virtually none have the deep trash middens and numerous burials characteristic of long-occupied villages. Mimbres bowls were precious in the eleventh century, so the quantity found indicates these sites were closely bound to the Mimbres homeland.

During the eleventh century Mimbres society heaved in one relatively brief spasm of expansion across the basinlands of south-central New Mexico. Life on its frontiers was precarious and few villages endured. By about A.D. 1150 the Classic Mimbres period had ended. Soon the gorgeous cream and black bowls were no longer available to the modest villages which hung on in the foothills of the Sierra Blanca and in the Chupadera Mesa country. For a time satisfactory copies were made locally to replace treasured heirlooms. Eventually, even these were broken, never to be replaced.

ONCE IT WAS "LAW EAST OF THE PECOS"!

Just a century ago, lands *west* of the Pecos were considered untamed. Ironically, around A.D. 1000, the situation was reversed. At that time, the Pecos Valley held New Mexico's *easternmost* outposts of civilized village life.

Although small family bands had camped and hunted within sight of the river for six thousand years between late Paleo-Indian times and A.D. 800, settled village life came late to the valley of the Pecos. Mere traces of the first farming settlements built between Alamogordo Reservoir and Roswell have been discovered. During the 1950s the earliest of these were found south of Fort Sumner on terraces overlooking the river's "18 Mile Bend." Gray, unpainted Anasazi pottery from northwestern New Mexico and scattered fragments of stone dart points mark these sites. By A.D. 1000, late "18 Mile" sites were well-established and more numerous. A few shallow, dugout "pithouses" and remnants of small mud-and-cobble-walled surface rooms have been excavated. Although everyday brown pottery was made locally, striking "Red Mesa Black-on-white" bowls, first made in the Red Mesa Valley near Gallup, were traded to the Pecos district from west of the Rio Grande.

As Anasazi and Mogollon population exploded in western New Mexico, Classic Chaco and Mimbres societies were formed and resources stretched to their limits. Pioneers were forced to seek new farmlands on the raw eastern frontier across the Rio Grande. These early settlers moved into territory that nomadic Indian plainsmen had always dominated. The villagers' economic and cultural ties were with western New Mexico, but life was hard and often isolated.

For a time, about A.D. 1050, Pecos villages were larger and more densely populated. During the time known as the "Mesita Negra" Period more farming hamlets were created in a century than in all other periods combined. Trade was far-flung.

"Mesita Negra" villages obtained Mimbres pottery from Grant, Sierra, and Luna Counties in southwestern New Mexico. "Reserve Black-on-white" pitchers were carried nearly three hundred miles from Catron County, while "Cebolleta Black-on-white" pottery came from Cibola and Valencia Counties south of Acoma Pueblo. "Socorro Black-on-white" bowls and ladles also found their way east across the Rio Grande.

Even so, the district was poor when compared to towns in the Chaco and Mimbres heartlands. Virtually nothing was discarded until beyond repair and unbroken prehistoric pottery is almost never found in the Pecos district. Harvests were smaller and no great granaries have ever been unearthed. Wild plant foods supplemented the corn harvest. In some areas acorns from scrubby "shinnery oak" were collected and ground into paste. Grass seeds, berries, and the carbohydrate-rich hearts of mescal cactus were all prized. Large game was very scarce—as it was throughout the Southwest between A.D. 1050 and 1100. What meat there was came primarily from rabbits, tortoises, prairie dogs, mice, ground-squirrels, and even lizards.

After A.D. 1100, when hard times came to Classic Chaco and Mimbres Society, the Pecos settlements began to create more of their own pottery types and economic attachments to western New Mexico evaporated. Great quantities of a cooking ware known as "Roswell Brown" were suddenly found in the Fort Sumner area, indicating the growth of strong social and economic networks along the length of the valley. Women made pottery; Fort Sumner Indian men were probably taking wives from the Roswell area.

A boldly decorated local pottery, "Chupadero Black-on-white," replaced western imports. It was manufactured at many villages from the White Sands and Mountainair on the west to Fort Sumner and Carlsbad on the east. The area around the charming present-day village of Lincoln was probably the geographic center of the vast Chupadero pottery country. Variations of this pottery were manufactured for centuries along the western approaches to the Pecos Valley.

But times change. By A.D. 1250 agricultural life was fading along the river and corn had become a rare harvest. Although not every inch of the Valley has been investigated, archeologists know of only four sites between Fort Sumner and Roswell which were inhabited during the A.D. 1200s. Virtually no fancy pottery wares were imported, but quantities of *Bison* bone have been found in each site.

About A.D. 1300, after decades of drought, *Bison* herds and tall grass reappeared along the Pecos, seducing local farmers to abandon the soil and turn to hunting. For five hundred years, between A.D. 1350 and 1850, buffalo camps —eventually including those of the Apache, Comanche, and Ute—replaced farmsteads along the middle Pecos River. Those who persisted in tilling the land first withdrew to the cool Sacramento highlands between Ruidoso and Corona. By A.D. 1400, most had again moved westward to the wide valley of the Rio Grande.

From historical accounts we know that New Mexico's surviving Pueblo farmers both feared and romanticized tribes of buffalo hunters on the eastern plains. No doubt they were both horrified and fascinated by a rough-and-tumble system of "Law *East* of the Pecos."

Prehistoric rock art: rattlesnakes and stars are common. Photograph by Rory P. Gauthier.

PART V

AFTER THE FALL
OF CHACO AND MIMBRES SOCIETY

Cliff dwelling in the Gila Wilderness. Drawing by Scott Andrae.

Chaco and Mimbres Society faded quickly. By A.D. 1150, thousands had fled the scrubby basins, seeking refuge in surrounding highlands. Many starved, some were raided, and the great trading networks disintegrated. Eventually, large villages were founded in forested areas like Mesa Verde and Bandelier National Monument, but drought came again in the late A.D. 1200s, forcing settlement along permanent rivers. About A.D. 1300, some who survived founded villages ancestral to the modern Pueblos.

HARD TIMES IN THE HIGHLANDS:
AFTER THE FALL OF CHACO AND MIMBRES SOCIETY

Classic Chacoan and Mimbres society was brilliant, vibrant —and brief. Beginning around A.D. 1100, after only 150 years of good times, decline set in. People moved out of the warm, scrubby basins to upland areas of mixed pinon/ponderosa forest where new farmsteads were built. Some groups resettled near long-abandoned villages in surrounding highlands, while others pioneered in remote, forested districts like the Upper Gila drainage or the area around Bandelier National Monument north of Santa Fe.

About four thousand sites of this "Upland Period" are known to archeologists. Many are food-gathering camps. Others are masonry pueblos of ten to fourteen rooms. Hundreds more are small villages of timber-roofed dugouts, or "pithouses"—a settlement pattern revived from two centuries earlier.

These villages tended to be very modest. Two deep pithouses surrounded by crude masonry storage rooms, often stockaded, were common. In northern New Mexico, a surprising number of these had been burned. Dismembered skeletons were found in the ruins—evidence of widespread social disorder in the A.D. 1100s following Chaco and Mimbres decline.

In the southern part of the state villages were larger, commonly four to six pithouses. Evidence of warfare is less dramatic in the Mimbres country and the defensive palisades rarely found.

Throughout New Mexico pithouse settlements of this period are found in cool, forested elevations averaging about 7,000 feet above sea level, though some have been found at 9,000 feet. In these locations, cold nighttime temperatures retarded crop development, so the food economy was based on a mix of hunting, foraging, and cultivating small garden plots. Many of these sites are hidden away in isolated mountain coves, and few trade goods are found in them. Social isolation and difficult times are indicated.

The re-introduction of pithouse settlements throughout New Mexico's forested districts is the most surprising characteristic of the "Upland Period." True, pithouse villages had

been built for nearly five hundred years prior to the development of the walled, often multistoried, pueblos of the Classic Chaco and Mimbres periods. But once these pueblos were developed, the pithouse was abandoned altogether as a house type—only to reappear again two centuries later almost simultaneously in each of New Mexico's cultural districts. Societies rarely "reverse" themselves and revive ancient ways of doing things.

Even more rarely do societies as distinct as those of the Mogollon (Mimbres) and Anasazi (Chacoan) simultaneously reverse themselves in so specific a way. Clearly, cold climates in the high country dictated pithouses —warm, easily heated, subterranean chambers, like bermed solar houses of today—as the most efficient solution to the housing needs of rapidly relocated villages.

The palisaded pithouse villages of the Gallina highlands are numerous and well-known. Most of these have been dated to between A.D. 1100 and A.D. 1200. Once considered anomalous, these are now understood as typical of a statewide architectural trend. In the Sierra Blanca area near Ruidoso, pithouse villages of this period are known as the "Late Glencoe" phase; in the Reserve area, as the "Apache Creek" phase. Pithouse villages were also common at A.D. 1200 in the upper Rio Grande, in the Taos district, and in the Zuni area.

In most places, pithouse construction was followed by the resurgence of moderately sized above-ground masonry pueblos. In the Sierra Blanca region, these villages are known as the early "Lincoln" phase. In Catron County, they are attributed to the "Tularosa" phase. Those in the Santa Fe and Los Alamos areas belong to the "Coalition" period.

Following the redevelopment of above-ground walled pueblos in the highlands, people again drew together and village size gradually increased. This increase was most notable between A.D. 1260 and 1280, near the end of the "Upland Period." Textbooks generally refer to these large, late period towns as "Pueblo III" or "Great Pueblo," but it is easier to think of them simply as villages of an "Upland Period" which lasted from about A.D. 1140 to A.D. 1290.

Left: Tyuonyi at Bandelier National Monument. Photograph by Tracey Morse.

77

Tyuonyi at Bandelier National Monument. Photograph by Tracey Morse.

Right: Long House at Bandelier National Monument. Photograph by
Tracey Morse.

Many are famous and quite impressive. Gila Cliff Dwelling, Tyuonyi at Bandelier, Cliff House at Mesa Verde, and Atsinna at El Morro are all well-known. The cliff-houses are dramatic but comparatively rare and not truly typical of the "Upland Period." The largest of the far more common pueblo-style villages might contain two hundred to four hundred ground-floor rooms, but the heyday of the largest ones span a surprisingly brief period between roughly A.D. 1220 and 1280. Many were constructed in the A.D. 1250s, only to be abandoned a mere decade or two later. Those that endured beyond the 1280s—among them Quarai, Tabira, and Casa Colorado between Mountainair and Claunch—were generally situated on the moist east slopes of major mountain masses.

Why did population shift to the highlands after the Classic Period? The early A.D. 1100s brought drought conditions and the decline of harvest surpluses to the late Chacoan and Mimbres villages. This led, in turn, to malnutrition and unsettled conditions. Because it was increasingly necessary to forage for wild foodstuffs, and because rainfall is greater in the mountains, entire local populations took refuge there. The early to mid-A.D. 1200s were more stable climatically, and large, well-known villages flourished at Mesa Verde and Bandelier. But the good times were brief.

The "Great Drought" of A.D. 1276–99 was felt all the way from Colorado to central Mexico's Aztec empire. Agriculture was severely disrupted and the forested districts once again abandoned. At the famous "Site 616" on Mariana Mesa north of Quemado, villagers simply walked away, leaving all their possessions in place. Throughout the cool highlands, cliff-houses fell silent, and cooking fires never again wafted their pungent haze into the steel-blue evening sky.

SITE 616, MARIANA MESA

Incessant spring winds suck at the gritty floor of Horse Camp Canyon where a dust devil swirls between clumps of sage and sparse, wind-blown junipers. The canyon cuts abruptly through a humpbacked ridge of volcanic rubble, skirts a miniature plateau—once the main plaza of an impressive Tularosa Period pueblo, then winds toward Route 17, the lonely road to Quemado.

Seven hundred years ago the prehistoric occupants of this village known as "Site 616," abandoned their home on the north flank of Mariana Mesa, leaving behind nearly all of their possessions. No one has ever discovered why because only a few poignant and conflicting clues remain.

Near an ancient wall several inhabitants had fallen to violence, but were never buried. In places, clay floors have been baked hard like pottery and charred roof beams attest to unchecked fires.

Elsewhere, a young girl had been killed with an axe-blow to her forehead, her right arm severed at the elbow, as she lingered on a roof top. The room below was then put to the torch. She fell, already dead, as the partly burned roof caved in, only to be rediscovered seven hundred years later—the remains of a delicate necklace of fine jet beads still at her throat. In spite of the violence, these beads are eloquent testimony that general looting, which inevitably followed the fall of so rich a village to armed victors, never came.

Like many other villages in the Zuni highlands, "Site 616" was founded about A.D. 1150. At that time people moved away from lower elevations in the Chaco Canyon district and into surrounding uplands. About 7,300 feet above sea level, easily defended and surrounded by forested mountains and mesas, "Site 616" was typical.

The village began modestly. First, several dugout pitrooms were excavated and roofed over with local timber. Later, linear blocks of cobble and adobe walled rooms were added, a few at a time. By about A.D. 1220 the village's outer walls enclosed a rectangle measuring 800 feet long by 650 feet wide. A modern football field would easily have fit inside the central plaza.

"Site 616" was constructed like a huge fort. No windows, doors, or city gates opened to its well-made exterior stone walls. By A.D. 1250 more than five hundred rooms faced the plaza, many entered only from ladders to the roof. Unlike large towns built 150 years earlier at Chaco Canyon, "Site 616" was but one story in height. A huge "D" shaped kiva, or underground ceremonial room, similar to those found today in the Rio Grande Pueblos, was located in one corner of the plaza.

In another area investigators found a real rarity. A thirty-foot oval had been excavated into the plaza's floor. This proved to be a spiral rampway and led down a dozen feet to a shallow well. "Site 616" had an emergency water supply in case of attack! At the well's bottom a dense layer of gray clay overlaid by sand trapped water seeping from the volcanic slope behind the pueblo. Clay from the well was also used to make much of the village's everyday cooking ware.

Corn was scarce, but bushels of other plant seeds—mostly from cactus and pigweed—were found. Unlike the meat-scarce diet of earlier Chaco and Mimbres villagers, discarded bones tell us that a more plentiful menu here consisted of pronghorn antelope, mule deer, bison, turkey, rabbit, and bighorn sheep.

In prehistoric New Mexico, essential tools such as stone mauls, drills, or arrowheads had to be painstakingly manufactured by hand. Even roof timbers, hand cut with inefficient stone axes, were usually too valuable to abandon. So the inhabitants of most settlements took away nearly every usable item, including building materials, when they migrated to new farmsteads or fled from attackers. Thus most archeological sites yield only fragments of broken and discarded artifacts.

But "Site 616" was different. Huge quantities of prehistoric artifacts were found in place, as if the populace had merely walked off one day, leaving behind all their possessions—a treasure trove of information about everyday life in the A.D. 1200s.

Quantities of jewelry and semi-precious stones were also found. Beetles, frogs, bats, and birds were created from shell, jet, turquoise, or reddish jaspers. Stone, bone, and shell beads were manufactured. Then, as now, fine cylindrically ground strands of "hishi" were highly prized. An ingenious variety of needles, awls, scrapers, whistles, finger rings, tubes, and figurines was fashioned from the bones of hunted animals.

Why would anyone walk away and leave all this? In the thirteenth century a stunning drought destroyed agriculture throughout the Southwest. Dozens of villages were abandoned nearly simultaneously, but most were stripped bare of valuables as folks drifted away. Was there simply no one left to claim "Site 616"'s prized possessions? We will probably never know.

It is an impressive view from the canyon rim. Arizona lies twenty-two empty miles due west. Below, arroyos with names like Whiskey Creek and Yankee Gulch wind along ponderosa-studded hills until they join Apache Creek. There, at 7,000 feet above sea level, one finds a forgotten piece of Catron County's remote past.

Thereabouts, the more recent past was so colorful that the names of local landmarks do not let one forget it. So Apache Canyon carries its stream south to the hamlet of Apache Creek at the Tularosa River. Seven miles northeast is Aragon, established in the 1870s as Fort Tularosa. Mount Apache pushes into the skyline. It does not take much genius to figure out that this area was an Apache Indian stronghold just over a century ago.

Yet it was not always that way. It is easy to forget that the various Apache bands only held dominion over this country for two, perhaps three, centuries. Earlier, Mogollon settlers along Apache Creek did better. They built—and rebuilt—villages there for a thousand years.

The Museum of New Mexico began excavation in 1971 to salvage archeological sites threatened by road improvements along State Route 32. David Kaiser directed the project. Excavation foreman Regge Wiseman, now Assistant State Archeologist, recently reported findings on this little-known area.

Although Apache Creek's "golden age" came in the A.D. 1200s, after the decline of Classic Chaco and Mimbres villages, Mogollon families first settled there about A.D. 300. They built dugout pithouses on natural terraces above the creek. Their pithouses were oval or bean-shaped and excavated to a depth of roughly three feet. They were roofed with timber, bark, and banked soil—reminiscent of old Navajo hogans.

Archeologists term this period the "Pine Lawn Phase." Pottery was an undecorated earthenware called "Alma Plain." Villagers farmed small corn plots along the creek bottom and collected wild foods to supplement their harvest. At Apache Creek these settlements typically consisted of two or three pithouses. At several, very large pit structures

Three circle neck-banded cooking olla–about A.D. 900. Drawing by Scott Andrae.

were found. These may have been early ceremonial houses, or kivas.

Later pithouses, constructed about A.D. 700, tended to be square rather than oval. These usually contained storage cists or chambers, some dug into room floors. Numerous storage bins indicated that agricultural harvests were larger and more important than in earlier times. These settlements belong to the "San Francisco Phase"—named after ruins containing a well-made red pottery first found along the San Francisco River.

"San Francisco" pithouses were occupied over a considerable span of time and were continually renovated. Archeologists found multiple packed earth floors which they peeled away like the layers of an onion.

The last pithouse villages built on Apache Creek belong to the "Three Circle Phase," about A.D. 850. Similar villages are also found throughout the Mimbres country. These generally average twenty-five shallow, rectangular pithouses, although larger ones exist. However, at Apache Creek "Three Circle" villages were small. Pithouses were oval, seldom plastered inside, and quickly abandoned.

84

Within a century even more differences emerged between northern Catron County villages and those in the south. In the Mimbres region, large "Three Circle" villages were still being constructed when the first masonry foundations of above-ground pueblos were laid along Apache Creek. Similar "Reserve Phase" pueblos are scattered throughout northern Catron and western Socorro counties. At these, black-on-white pottery was produced at a time when red-on-white was still in vogue farther south. Masonry architecture and black-on-white pottery are considered as characteristic of northern New Mexico's ancient Anasazi people—not the Mogollon, so three generations of archeologists have argued over how these characteristics came to Catron County. Some say Anasazi people "migrated"; others that the Mogollon and Anasazi merely traded across their frontiers.

Back on Apache Creek, no one in the "Reserve" villages intended to become the subject of robust scholarly debate a thousand years later. Folks just carried on as best they could. Times were not easy. Masonry rooms were often repaired, renovated, and abandoned—only to be repaired and used again. At one site near Yankee Gulch, dismembered skeletons were found scattered about. Such evidence of conflict is widespread in New Mexico during the A.D. 1100s.

Conditions then stabilized for a time. Large-roomed pueblos of the Tularosa Period, about A.D. 1200-1300, were built near earlier village sites along Apache Creek. Excavations at these yield impressive numbers of *manos* and *metates*, essential corn-grinding implements.

Several Tularosa Period sites were deeply buried by eroded soil from the slopes of Apache Canyon. Thus preserved, they also yielded layer after layer of renovated room floors. Deep hearths, well-used ash pits, and remodelling of masonry walls indicate that successive generations managed a delicate balance on Apache Creek.

Carefully terraced gardens were also created. In one, on the hill above a "Tularosa" pueblo, rows of Agave still grow! Far from its native range, the Agave is mute testimony to agricultural engineering eight hundred years ago.

By A.D. 1300 the forested uplands of west-central New Mexico were abandoned. Until then, a lot of living had gone on in that one canyon—a thousand years of building, hoping, toiling, and dying—all before the Apache came to Apache Creek.

Steep rubble mounds encircle the forgotten plaza, creating a shadowed hollow where winter's chill clings to crusted patches of snow. Only fifty yards away a breeze rises from the sun-warmed stone of the mesa's south face, then rushes through tall ponderosas, rattling dead branches overhead. Like the air that reaches it a mile and one-third above sea level, the mesa's soil is thin and brittle. Yet it once supported a prehistoric pueblo large enough to include two central plazas and three massive house mounds, each several stories tall. There were more than four hundred rooms on the ground floors and five kivas, or subterranean ceremonial chambers. Deep and circular, these were laboriously pecked out of the mesa's bedrock with stone hand chisels—mute testimony to lavish reverence for religious tradition, even in adversity.

The evidence of adversity is everywhere. Thumbnail-sized fragments of pottery place the village in a time period between A.D. 1230 and 1290—almost surely built and abandoned in the span of a single lifetime. Even the chert nodules from which sharp flakes were once struck away to create stone tools have been worked down to stingy nubbins. And back in the ponderosas, long walls built of rough stone blocks and cobbles, then faced with dirt, created a reservoir which trapped precious rainwater as it flowed down the sloping tongue of the narrow mesa.

In spite of the reservoir there were times of want. One section of the main houseblock's steep east wall has fallen away to expose parts of human skeletons, once properly buried in masonry niches. Many of the bones are thin and porous. Chronic malnutrition and calcium deficiencies had induced the degenerative bone condition known as osteoporosis.

This prehistoric ruin, designated LA 12,700 in New Mexico's series of more than 40,000 numbered archeological sites, is but one of thousands scattered throughout the high Pajarito Plateau on lands belonging to the Santa Fe National Forest and Bandelier National Monument. Some house mounds are smaller and older, built in the A.D. 1100s.

Cave rooms on the Pajarito Plateau. Photograph by Tracey Morse.

Others, like the gracefully circular ruin of Tyuonyi at Bandelier, were founded about A.D. 1300 along permanent streams in the lower canyons and flourished for many generations. This rugged canyon and mesa country between the crest of the Jemez Mountains and the Rio Grande is less well known archeologically than many realize. Thousands of ruins remain to be discovered and properly recorded. On average, archeologists have found twenty sites, large and small, in each square mile that has been surveyed on foot. Careful investigation of such rugged country is slow, painstaking work. The Pajarito's quarter of a million acres may hold as many as seven thousand archeological sites. Yet, in a century of research only a third of these have actually been located and numbered. Fewer than two hundred have been excavated, most prior to the development of modern laboratory and dating techniques. Still, the area around Bandelier National Monument has offered up enough of its ancient secrets to tell a remarkable story.

Until the A.D. 1100s, the high, forested mesa country around Bandelier National Monument was empty save for occasional hunting parties and expeditions to quarry the Jemez Caldera's glassy obsidian, prized for arrowheads. But events that would eventually bring many refugee families to the Pajarito had already been set into motion more than a hundred miles to the west. After the fall of Chaco and Mimbres society some starved, others were raided, and many retreated into hidden mountain coves, returning to a hunting and foraging economy.

Existing highland peoples in the Gallinas area between Cuba and Lindrith were particularly hard hit by the outward collapse of Chacoan society. There, the archeological evidence of tragedy can be found in full measure. Pithouses were laboriously dug into the tongues of high mesas then completely palisaded. Sometimes a stockade's postholes were hand ground into the solid sandstone of a high promontory. But even these defenses were invariably breached, and most settlements were looted and burned. Decapitated skeletons, including those of children, are common. Archeologists know little of the raider's identity. In some cases different tribal groups probably came to blows; in others, local clans may have turned on one another.

Left: Cave rooms at LA 12,700. Photograph by Rory P. Gauthier.

Across the barrier of the Jemez Caldera, the Pajarito country seems to have escaped the worst torments of the mid-A.D. 1100s. But someday someone will inevitably discover and excavate unexpected pithouses of the A.D. 1100s in the remote and largely unstudied higher canyons at Bandelier National Monument. By A.D. 1175, conditions had settled down throughout the highlands and a number of small masonry pueblos were founded on the Pajarito. Most are simple but nicely constructed houseblocks, often two rows deep, generally with ten to twenty rooms. Unlike houseblocks of later periods, nearly all of these were built in areas where there are ponderosa or mixed ponderosa and piñon forests.

Although not spectacular and seldom pointed out to park visitors, literally hundreds of these small pueblos have been found over the years. Their construction coincides with the introduction of a distinctive painted pottery known as "Santa Fe Black-on-white." Santa Fe Black-on-white actually has a gray background decorated with "ghosty" black designs. The designs are painted in carbon black, then fired, unlike Chaco-Anasazi pottery's mineral (usually oxides of iron) painted decorations.

About A.D. 1200, "cliff-houses" appeared in mountain areas scattered across four states. Among the most famous and most adored sites in the Southwest, they are also among the rarest. For every cliff-house, whether at Mesa Verde, Bandelier, or elsewhere, there are probably a hundred less spectacular, contemporaneous masonry houseblocks to be found within a few miles. At Bandelier, Long House and Talus House were founded at this time, although renovated for generations afterwards.

There are many explanations for the development of the delightful cliff-house style of architecture. A very sensible one is that the high country where they were built is quite cold for many months of the year. Cliff-houses face *south* or southwest, occasionally southeast. They soak up heat from the low winter sun and store it, just as would an immense passive solar building of today.

Those many hundreds of shovel-shaped "cavate," or hand carved cave rooms in the cliffs above sites like Tyuonyi and Otowi at Bandelier and at Puye also face south and are undoubtedly warm, wintertime shelters. Many tourist brochures suggest that some families simply preferred to live in these.

90

Upland Pueblo built into a cliff face—once several stories tall.
Photograph by Tracey Morse.

It is much more likely that in severe winters most families retreated to either one of these or to the warmth of the deep kivas, like those where early Spanish explorers wintered at Zuñi. Site LA 12,700 on its high, cold mesa also had cave rooms carved out of its south face, just below the pueblo.

For a time in the mid-A.D. 1200s, larger masonry pueblos flourished on the Pajarito. Like "Site 616" at Mariana Mesa, these were usually in the upper reaches of the piñon zone, a bit lower in elevation than the small, early Santa Fe Black-on-white houseblocks. Corn agriculture again flourished and villages continued to grow larger.

Then came the "Great Drought" of A.D. 1276–99. The high east slopes of mountain ranges are moister than are west slopes. Albuquerque residents have only to compare the relatively harsh west face of the Sandias with the verdant, rolling forests of the east slope. Because the Pajarito faced east, villages there weathered the horrendous droughts far better than those on the west slopes of the Jemez Mountains where large pueblos in the Gallinas highlands fifty miles west of Los Alamos fell silent for all time. But many on the Pajarito survived, resorting to mesa-top reservoirs and small cobbles used as moisture retaining "mulch" on neatly laid out garden plots.

As the drought deepened, it may also have gotten colder.

Climatologists sometimes refer to the A.D. 1250-1500 period as a "little ice-age." Eventually, harsh conditions forced even the hardiest to abandon the highest mesas. LA 12,700 was abandoned, as were a thousand other pueblos in New Mexico's higher mountains. It was time to move to the permanent streams in lower canyons. So Tyuonyi flourished.

However, by A.D. 1300 or 1325, Puebloan peoples had largely retreated to the lower lands along the Rio Grande and its major tributaries, and the creative focus of prehistoric society shifted out of the lovely uplands. In the 1400s and early 1500s there were fewer villages, but many were immense, often a thousand rooms or more. From time to time drought or clan disputes, particularly about A.D. 1500, temporarily drove some families again to the cool mesa country. The people of Jemez in particular repeatedly withdrew to their private mesa-top strongholds.

For centuries descendants of many mountain villages on the Pajarito tended shrines or occasionally renovated a kiva. But many villages died out altogether, so particular ancestral places were sometimes forgotten. That is what happened at LA 12,700. Yet the strong hands that so carefully created five perfect kivas from solid bedrock nearly seven hundred years ago would have been pleased with today. The sky is still the color of the most precious turquoise, the cave rooms below the mesa's rim are sunlit, the soil is moist, and an eagle circles directly overhead.

THE RIVERINE PERIOD:
ROOTS OF MODERN PUEBLO SOCIETY

The Riverine Period, a time of radical change between A.D. 1300 and 1540, followed the heyday of upland villages. Except in the Hopi country of Arizona, dry-farming was generally abandoned for the security of modest irrigation systems created on low-lying flood plains. New religious patterns were established, and the Kachina Cult, associated with masked gods and rainmaking, spread to the Rio Grande from the southwest.

The earliest Riverine pueblos were usually small, ten to fifty rooms, and built on easily fortified bluffs above the Rio

Macaw petroglyph near Albuquerque—the bird's feathers were highly prized in late prehistoric times. Photograph by Cynthia M. Stuart.

Standing wall at the Galisteo Pueblo of San Cristobal. Photograph by Rory P. Gauthier.

Grande and adjacent streams. Black-on-white pottery styles passed out of vogue and were replaced by elaborate glaze-wares. Black-on-red was the dominant color scheme, but other variations are known.

What caused such sweeping changes? The "Great Drought" of A.D. 1276–99 utterly destroyed agriculture and food reserves in the Southwest's great upland villages, even those at Mesa Verde. Only a handful—invariably located in high, well-watered canyons like Tyuonyi in Bandelier National Monument—were spared.

For more than a quarter of a century, the Southwest sizzled under virtually rainless skies! Eventually, even the most tenacious villagers abandoned their tinder-dry uplands and began small settlements in lower elevations along New Mexico's permanent streams.

By A.D. 1325 survivors had concentrated along the Rio Grande and Rio San Jose in the Acoma area, as well as on the Chama, Zuni, and Gila Rivers. Some lesser creeks like the Galisteo were also settled. Villages ancestral to the modern Pueblos were founded—often within a few miles of today's village sites.

The densest concentration of settlements was along the Rio Grande between San Marcial and Taos. But conditions were not stable, for the river sometimes carried away entire farmsteads and uninterrupted habitation at any one location

A "field house" of the Riverine Period. Photograph by Rory P. Gauthier.

was uncommon. In southern New Mexico, massive adobe villages, called "Saladoan," were built along the Gila River. They had already been abandoned by Spanish times so comparatively little is known about them.

By the early 1400s villages had grown larger. They were often built out on the flood plains and defense was not so important. While fewer in number than the early Riverine villages, some grew to immense proportions. The largest contained two to three thousand ground-floor rooms and positively dwarf the more famous sites such as Pueblo Bonito at Chaco Canyon. A contemporary football stadium could easily be fit into the largest plazas at these great towns.

One particularly impressive cluster of late prehistoric pueblos lies along Galisteo Creek southeast of Santa Fe. The largest Galisteo villages include Pueblo She', Galisteo, Las Madres, and San Cristobal. Another Galisteo village, Pueblo Colorado, is smaller, but was constructed entirely of hand-matched red sandstone blocks. It consists of about a thousand ground-floor rooms arranged in eleven massive room blocks enclosing eight plazas.

Village size peaked about A.D. 1425, and none larger were ever built. But even in that period, the population of these massive towns fluctuated from season to season. Most were surrounded by many square miles of one- and two-room farmsteads. Called "field houses" by archeologists, these were

95

used during the agricultural season. Once a town's size reached a certain point, traveling to the farthest agricultural fields each day was no longer practical.

In the late A.D. 1400s many villages were temporarily vacated. Unstable agricultural conditions—alternating floods and droughts—forced relocations throughout the river districts as entire clans sought new farmlands. Large-cobbed corn, squash, beans, melons, and various herbs provided the mainstay of daily diet. Domestic turkey supplemented deer, buffalo, bighorn sheep, and other large game, but community rabbit hunts provided the most commonly eaten meat.

Locally grown cotton was used to weave both beautifully made *mantas* and everyday clothing. Handcrafts of all kinds— pottery, basketry, tools, and turquoise jewelry—were well-made and traded over large districts. Turquoise mines near present day Cerrillos—laboriously hand-worked with stone tools for many centuries—supplied an important source of wealth and influence. Local turquoise was carried down the long trade routes to central Mexico, and some Aztec Period artworks contain turquoise from the Cerrillos mine.

The Riverine Period was undoubtedly the high-point of large village life in New Mexico, but the region-wide political system of the earlier Chacoan Period did not reappear. River populations were divided into relatively small, often competing, local districts. Continual village relocations eventually divided groups speaking the same language.

When the Spanish arrived in 1540–41, Piro-speaking people lived along the Rio Grande from Los Lunas south to San Marcial. Tewa speakers, ancestors of today's Sandia and Isleta Pueblos, held the river between Bosque Farms and Bernalillo. To the north Tiwa, Tewa, Towa, and Tanoan speakers had fragmented into even smaller districts. Keresan people, then as now, lived both along the Rio Grande and in the Acoma-Laguna area, and many villages dotted the region around Zuni Pueblo, the only one in that region to survive.

Sadly, two centuries of intermittent famine, warfare, disease, and dislocation followed the Chacoan decline, erasing the details of subsequent migrations and all but a few half-remembered legends of earlier days. For decades, archeologists have tried in vain to trace today's pueblos directly back to Chaco Canyon and to determine just who lived there in the A.D. 1000s. To date, the confirmed roots of today's pueblos reach no further back in time than A.D. 1250 or 1300.

EPILOGUE

WALKING WEST—
A DAY'S WORK IN SOUTHWESTERN ARCHEOLOGY

We have been walking due west for nearly two and a half hours. Our shadows race before us, the morning sun at our backs. To my right walks John Broster. Years ago, we were classmates in graduate school, worked together, and visited archeological sites in Mexico.

Now a client is paying us to investigate a hundred-mile-long pipeline right-of-way. The law requires us to locate, record, and identify all archeological remains. This involves no high technology. We simply walk every foot of it.

So, John and I are still out looking for ancient sites—just two shadows cut down to size by the mid-morning sun. Mid-morning and it's time for a break!

We pull off our packs and drop down on a grassy clearing by a piñon. Now there is time to rest and examine our surroundings. Hunting for archeological sites, our eyes constantly sweep the ground before us, alert for pottery fragments, scatters of stone flakes, or low mounds of the oblong sandstone building blocks that indicate an Anasazi ruin. We rarely look up.

We are about 7,300 feet above sea level and have been walking all morning on a long, gently sloping mesa. The surrounding country is studded with piñon and juniper trees, gray-green and dark green against a cloudless, turquoise sky. The red-brown soil, rocky and dry, is broken here and there by patches of grama grass and rabbitbrush.

John pulls out the huge crinkled tangle of air photos and topographic maps he has crammed into his backpack. Where are we? Always we need to know. We find our little clearing on the photographs and interpolate our location onto the map. It is only a mile uphill to the Continental Divide. Beyond lies the descent into scorching sand country. John taps anxiously on his snuff tin before restoring it to the side pocket of his faded blue field jacket. He always does that when it is time to get moving.

We take up positions about forty feet apart. Climbing toward the Continental Divide, our boots crunch steadily in the dry, rocky soil. Gradually our eyes take over while sounds and body movements recede into a dreamy, rhythmic distance. The ground at our boot tips is very vivid—a miniature world of sticks and grass, fractured pebbles, bits of juniper stump, even the filter tip of a cigarette smoked long ago.

What's this? A spot of clear gray disrupts the red-brown color scheme of this miniature world. It is a fragment of a prehistoric cooking pot, made by Anasazi farming people nine hundred years ago. Thumbnail-sized, smooth on one side but "corrugated" on the other, tiny ridges have been pinched from built up coils of clay to decorate the outside. John has taken off his pack.

Between us lies an uneven hillock of rough sandstone chunks, each about half the size of a cinderblock. Clumps of rabbitbrush have blurred the linear bases of ancient sandstone walls. We are standing on the remains of a small Anasazi pueblo.

We must formally record the site and have printed forms for everything: pottery—its design, color, paste, and temper; characteristics of stone tools and fragments; architecture; and environment. Grabbing bundles of orange surveyor's flags we encircle the site, placing them every few feet along the outside perimeter of visible artifacts.

With surveyor's tapes and Brunton compass, the tiny rubble mound is measured and mapped. Only 26 feet in length by 18 feet in width, it encloses barely 468 square feet, the size of a modest studio apartment. Some of its sandstone blocks have been scavenged for the foundation of a nearby Navajo hogan, also in ruins. The pueblo originally consisted of three or four small rooms—an isolated farmstead just large enough for one or two families.

Apparently the site was but briefly inhabited. Only three more pottery fragments are found: one of "Escavada Black-on-white"; one of "Gallup Black-on-white"; and one of "Chaco Corrugated" like the one first seen as we approached the ruin. These ceramics were all common between A.D.

Right: Survey Archeology: "a miniature world of twigs, pebbles and pottery shards." Photograph by Rory P. Gauthier.

1040 and 1100, the heyday of huge villages in Chaco Canyon National Monument, fifty miles to the north.

John has gone off to collect flaked stone fragments—debris from the manufacture of drills, arrowheads, and other tools. He inspects his finds with a powerful pocket lens, taking notes before replacing each fragment. We take nothing away. Everything is analyzed on the spot and left where found. Before leaving, a steel marking stake is driven deep into the rocky soil. Affixed to it is a small tag which reads "OCA:SUG:17:7/'76." "OCA" stands for the Office of Contract Archeology at the University of New Mexico. "SUG" is a project code name. This is the seventeenth site found on this project, and the date found is July, 1976. Later, our data forms are sent to the State Museum where our site will become known as LA (Laboratory of Anthropology, Santa Fe) 14,275—the fourteen thousand two-hundred seventy-fifth archeological site found in New Mexico.

The steel marking stake is the archeologist's own way of saying "Kilroy was here." Our job at this site is done, but the worst lies ahead. For the next thirty miles we'll follow sand dunes and scorching brick-red cliffs all the way to Gallup.

"Tap! Tap!" John signals with the snuff tin. He has packed, so we start up the hill. It is 11:20 a.m. I hear the steady crunch of my boots again. It is getting very hot, and my shadow is short.

I look up to my right. John is looking my way; he smiles and waves. Humans have trod this soil for ten thousand years. This is big country and the sheer expanse of it is intimidating. It is good to have a friend.

I smile to myself and the ground before me becomes vivid again. My boot sounds fade as I concentrate on twigs and grass and broken rock. God, it's hot! Twigs and grass and broken rock. Odd, my boots begin to sound louder. Then it hits me: heels crunch louder going downhill! We have crossed the Continental Divide. Here, water runs west.

"Hey, John, we're over the top. How long till we're out of the trees?"

"Couple hundred yards, I'd guess. How are you holding up, Pops?"

"Pretty well, for an old man of thirty-one."

"Good. We'll be able to fry eggs on our boots soon."

I wish he hadn't said that. I hadn't noticed before, but my feet are already swelling as the heat radiates through the soles of my boots.

The trees are smaller and more widely scattered now. We are on a large flat area that slopes gently to the south. Here we find an early Navajo log hogan, site number 18. We record it and move on. Five more minutes and we are out of the trees. Before us lies the Red Mesa Valley. From a distance the striking brick-red cliffs appear solid, lifeless, and remote. They keep watch over Interstate 40 for nearly thirty miles east of Gallup and give the wide Red Mesa Valley its name.

But today our view is far more intense. We have stopped on the rolling west face of a low, piñon-studded mesa, and the Valley lies directly below. Not 500 yards to the right, sheer cliffs shimmer in the staggering midday heat that rises from the Valley's sands. Awed by this landscape, we rest.

Several hundred feet high and flat as a billiard table on top, the red rock is piled up like a fantastic garden wall and runs due west as far as the eye can see. Gallup lies beyond.

Immense talus slopes protrude from the base of the wall, a jumble of sand, soil, and boulders scoured from the mesa by countless freezes and rains. Below, sizzling sand dunes and blotchy soils carpet the Valley. It looks like an ancient painter's cloth, stained—wrinkled--torn. The tears are deep, treacherous arroyos.

I can barely make out traffic moving along Interstate 40, about four miles to my left. Here, the highway parallels the Santa Fe Railway. This afternoon we will see heavy freight trains pass below us, to our left. With luck we'll see sunlight flashing from the polished parlor cars of the Superchief as it carries tourists west to California.

Nowadays the Red Mesa country is barren and sparsely populated. Yet less than a thousand years ago, this Valley was one of the Anasazi world's most prosperous farming districts.

Beginning in the late A.D. 800s, dozens of small farmsteads sprang up in the area of Fort Wingate, and many eventually grew into true villages. Within a century locally produced pottery, called "Red Mesa Black-on-white," was being traded over an area of several thousand square miles. The Valley's economic influence was felt at Chaco Canyon, sixty miles to the north.

By A.D. 1100, the good times had waned and other areas to the north and west became more important trading centers. But the Red Mesa Valley had already played out its role as an important crucible in the development of Puebloan farming society.

Our rest break is over. John has the binoculars and is focusing on the valley below to locate the bits of blue surveyor's flagging that we will follow into the afternoon sun. I tie a bandana around my forehead to keep streams of perspiration from clouding my vision.

As John and I descend, we see nothing save sand, rocks, and streaks of clay. Only an occasional clump of grass or rabbitbrush breaks the monotony. After nearly an hour's downhill walk we reach an old sand dune, stabilized by the roots of stubby grass and stunted juniper bushes. We slow down. These ancient dunes are likely places in which to discover archeological sites.

Sure enough! Within minutes we have located a scatter of pottery fragments. On some there are coarse black and white geometric designs. Others are crudely corrugated gray everyday wares, mixed with several fragments of another type which is smoothed on the exterior. This is an early site.

I look over my shoulder and see John lying on his belly, facing east. He catches my glance.

"I should'a known!" he says. "Darn near missed it with the sun in our eyes."

Now I'm on my belly too. We are both staring at ground level across a very shallow oval depression! About ten feet across, it is the remnant of a subterranean pithouse—carved out of the soil before the Anasazi built their houseblocks above ground.

Rory Gauthier, the third member of our team, arrives in the pickup while we are still engrossed. Today it is his turn to drive the supply truck while John and I walk. Rory is young and lean and possesses a naturally casual air that cloaks hawklike powers of observation. Born in Los Alamos, and one of the best field archeologists in the American Southwest, he has made a lifelong study of prehistoric pottery. Minutes later he returns with a handful of fragments.

"Yes, looks good! The Black-on-whites are a mixture of late 'Kiatuthlanna' and very early 'Gallup' styles. The plainware isn't much, but I'd say A.D. 800 to 950 for the lot."

This small farmstead dates from the Valley's first agricultural blossoming. Usually, only one large family lived at such a site, working nearby garden plots. In the warm seasons, daily activity centered on outdoor *ramadas*, or branch lean-to's, now long gone. Winters were spent in the warmth and safety of the deep pithouses. Hunting and collecting wild vegetal foods was an important supplement to harvests of corn, beans, and squash.

It is time for lunch, so John repositions our pickup truck. That way we can sit on the east side of its bed in a stingy patch of shade. Later in the day we will cross deep arroyos, seeking the remains of larger villages built in the eleventh century. But for the moment the luxuries of shade, cool tea, and food seem more important.

We decide on peanut butter and jelly sandwiches, but can't find the peanut butter.

I call to Rory, "Hey, have you seen the peanut butter? Did we forget to bring it?"

"No. It's in the bed of the truck getting all nice and gooey."

I should have remembered! Rory likes it that way. John digs through odds and ends, retrieving a jar filled with a substance resembling turgid honey. Suddenly, looking pained, he swears wickedly and reaches for his bandana. Already burned, John uses the folded bandana to twist off the jar's scorching hot lid. We pour the peanut butter onto sourdough buns—no utensils are necessary. It is even thinner than honey. Rory joins us as we end our meal. John asks him how things look ahead.

"Not good. There are wide arroyo cuts that I can't cross with the truck, and the road is undercut ahead as it rounds the edge of this dune. I'm going to have to leave you. I'll get to the highway somehow and go back in on the other side of these arroyos."

We consult the maps and decide to meet about four miles ahead at a place where a dirt road winds in from the Ciniza refinery. In preparation I stuff several oranges into each of our packs. John fills an extra canteen so we will have three between us. Our government maps are more than twenty years old; if that road no longer exists, we are going to have a rough day.

It is time to change clothes. Into the truck goes my undershirt, morning's socks, and stocking cap. Out come clean socks, a wide-brimmed Panama hat bought in Ecuador, and a lightly-woven, long-sleeved cotton and wool shirt. It is worn tails out. I tie a large blue bandana in a triangle over my head and drip water on it. The Panama goes on top of that.

John is making similar preparations. The truck's radio is tuned to Gallup, blaring the tune to "I Want to Hold Your Hand" with the lyrics sung in Navajo. I wonder to myself if the Beatles have ever heard this version of their classic. It is two o'clock. The radio announces news and weather, 106 degrees in downtown Gallup—heart of the Navajo Country." Lord! We are going to be fried like potato chips before this day is over!

Rory is ready to go. John and I decide to walk behind the truck as he attempts to negotiate the washed-out road just ahead. A hundred yards from us the road sweeps in a tight curve along the lip of the hill. But it is not an ordinary road—water churning over bare soil has undercut it by a distance of two or three feet. All that remains is a fragile shelf which juts out from the side of the hill.

Oh, my God! Gauthier is scarcely onto the ledge and the roadway is already crumbling. We are going to lose the pickup! Suddenly the motor roars and the truck plunges forward, tilting rakishly. For ten or twelve seconds Rory skims along the fractured ledge as it literally vanishes beneath him. Finally, the truck bottoms out on solid ground and disappears around the base of the hill, gone in a puff of blowing sand.

Transfixed, John and I are slow to notice that we have company. An old Navajo shepherd has been standing on the hill above tending his flock. Gold teeth are flashing in a wonderful grin as he nods his head appreciatively and waves his walking stick. A good "truck-man" is highly regarded here in Navajo Country. When snow and ice vanish in the spring melts, ten thousand square miles of Navajo Nation turn to impassable gumbo, and thousands of families are trapped in hogans, each many miles from nowhere. In these times, the government must use helicopters to drop food and prevent starvation. And strong men must walk out to give notice that old "so-and-so" lies mortally ill forty miles across the glassy clay. Sometimes the helicopters do not come in time. Yes, a good hand with a truck is highly regarded here. The old man waves his stick again, grins once more, and vanishes.

John and I move on. There is no crunching of boots now. Occasionally I hear the little shower of sand that is kicked up by a lazy step. Later, as I tire out and drag my feet, I will hear it continually.

There appear to be no sites in this wasteland, not even small scatters of artifacts. Yet the valley was once farmed. "Hey, John. How come we're not getting sites in here? Do you suppose they are thirty feet down?"

"You mean covered by alluvium from the mesa? Yes, I think so. We'll find out soon enough. The first big arroyo is just ahead."

In ten minutes we reach it. Good grief! The arroyo looks to be twenty feet to the bottom—loose sand all the way. There is a special technique for going down. I turn sideways so one shoulder is to the wall of the arroyo, hold the edge, and lean into the wall. I dig my heels into the sand with the outside leg extended; my inside heel is dug in with that leg half-extended. Now I simply let go and arrive on the arroyo floor in an avalanche of sand. Nothing to it!

We explore the arroyo bottom. Sure enough, there are traces of charcoal and bits of pottery in one wall where solid soil has been exposed. There are sites in this area, but many must be covered by ten to fifteen feet of soil washed down from the mesa and those massive talus slopes.

Getting out of the arroyo is not as easy as getting in. Again, the loose sand requires elán. But John Broster isn't a legend in this business for nothing. He is prepared. Out of his pack comes a collapsible army surplus trenching tool. Because no handholds can be gotten into the loose sand, John plunges the blade in deep and pulls himself up a few feet, repeating the operation. Eventually he disappears over the top with, "Heads up!"

I retrieve the little shovel and repeat the operation. It takes me several attempts. On the final one I start to slip just as I near the top, but strong arms grab me and pull me to solid ground. I am grateful. It has taken me ten minutes of exertion to get out of the hole.

We rest a few minutes and sip at our canteens. It is important to drink small amounts of water every fifteen minutes or so to prevent dehydration. I am crusted with perspiration and take a salt tablet, risking the nausea that sometimes follows. This is no place to faint in your own tracks.

105

We move on. I pull the Panama further down over my eyes. It is 3:30, and the afternoon sun is blinding. We slog on through the sand nearly a mile to the second major arroyo. No sites at all. It is 4:15 when we arrive, and I am tiring. We are low on water, and Gauthier is nowhere in sight. I ask John for the binoculars.

"Sorry, Pops, I had to give them back to Gauthier so he could spot us."

"Damn University! Do you think we'll ever work anywhere that has enough equipment?"

"Nope! Let's tackle the arroyo. If we stop now we won't have enough water to make it."

At 4:35 we are sitting on the arroyo's far bank, eating our oranges, but decide to save the remaining water. Ahead of us the soil is dark, hard, and veined like the back of your hand. It is an ancient clay surface, textured by unremembered rains. They came so long ago that no human was yet on this continent to watch the running water etch little furrows in the clay. Such a surface often traps artifacts because they are heavier than the overlying soil and sand, which is washed or blown away. This process leaves artifacts scattered on the surface, although one often can't tell much about how—or when —they were deposited. It is not uncommon to find artifacts which are separated by five thousand years lying together. This is easy walking after hours in the sand, but we find nothing.

Too quickly, we again reach soil mixed with sand and come upon a large scatter of pottery fragments. Stunted juniper, snakeweed, grama grass, and rabbitbrush dot a small knoll. Here we find Gallup Black-on-white and the same graywares as at the pithouse. We also find Red Mesa Black-on-white, which is named after this valley and was made between A.D. 900 and 1000. Unfortunately, we find no walls or hearths, no building stones, no housepits. So we record what we have and go on. My shadow, now tall and thin, follows me noiselessly.

There is yet another arroyo ahead. This one looks wide and deep like the first. Damn! At least we can see the Ciniza refinery to our left, so it cannot be too far to our rendezvous. John has stopped to look at a point on the right horizon, slightly above us. He pulls off his hat to shield his eyes and stares.

106

"I think there's someone on the other side of the arroyo."

"Really? I don't see anything."

"Well, *something* was out there 'cause I saw a spot of blue, but now it's gone."

"You don't think it might be Rory?" I ask, hopefully.

"We won't know till we get there, so let's get rolling." In five minutes we are sliding down another arroyo bank. The walls of this one hold nothing of interest.

"Hey, John, let's finish the water. I'm going to need it, or I'll never get to the top. I'm beat!"

"Maybe we'd better, my lips are cracking."

I save the last drop for the tip of my bandana and dab it luxuriously on my temples. Moments later, we find a spot in the far wall where a trail leads to the top. What luck! We needed a break.

After five minutes of dragging our feet through the sand, a log hogan materializes. It is partly hidden by a hill to the right. As we approach, a small frame-stucco house comes into view next to the hogan. A graded dirt road ends in the front yard. I am relieved.

"Ha! We've got a hogan and a road, but nothing BLUE. At least we can ask for water."

We are almost in front of the little stucco house when the door is flung open.

Broster grins in triumph. "Thought I was heat-crazed, didn't you?"

In the doorway stands a young Navajo girl. She is wearing bright blue pants and stares intently at us. She is curious, yet shy of strangers. We nod and smile but continue to stand where we are. Hereabouts, it is custom for visitors to wait outside for the host to come from the hogan.

As we stand there our tan pickup comes tooting up the road in a cloud of dust. Rory's head pops out of the cab.

"Hi guys, what took you so long?"

I retort, "We decided to walk in the shade, so we took the long way 'round."

Broster chuckles and makes a beeline for the water cooler. I am right on his heels. It takes me only ten minutes to absorb nearly three quarts of tea! It is lukewarm; I could care less.

Rory has started to tell us about a site on the hill ahead. "See it? It's just to the left of the old pipeline trench that cuts through the top of the hill. I was almost to the top checking out ceramics, but stayed on this slope so I could see you coming. There's plenty of sandstone up there. Let's record it before we knock off for the day."

It is nearly 5:30. We don't usually quit until about 6:00, so we decide to go ahead. Rory has already walked the survey line to the hill. We ride the next half-mile, resting swollen feet. It sure beats walking.

Reluctantly, we get out of the truck to record site number 21. Rory wasn't kidding; this is a dandy pueblo. There are unshaped sandstone blocks all over the hilltop. Let's see, the roomblock measures seventy feet, north-south by twenty-eight . . .

"Hey, John. Tighten up that tape, we don't have it straight."

"Right."

. . . it's thirty feet east-west. There are fourteen, fifteen, maybe seventeen rooms. There is a large, deep trash mound about sixty feet east of the main houseblock. Here we have a good ceramic inventory. There are some Black-on-red sherds. This means the site was built later in the Chacoan sequence than the ones with only Black-on-white pottery. Rory assigns dates of A.D. 1050–1150. There is no kiva, the circular subterranean ceremonial chamber common to most Chacoan sites. Perhaps we simply don't see it. John is driving in the site stake when I spot a large, distinctive fragment of Black-on-white pottery.

"Look, Rory. It's got large, black polka dots all over it! Have you ever seen any of this before?"

"No. Boy, that's neat stuff! Is there any more of it?"

"Just the one piece. You *really* haven't seen any before?

"Nope."

What a way to end the day! I have finally stumped Gauthier. Feeling expansive, I announce, "Quitting time. Sodas and beer on me."

We stroll down to the truck. Ten miles today. Not bad. Tonight we'll stay at the Shalimar Motel in Gallup. It is 6:34 p.m.—plenty of time for iced sodas and a long, cold shower before sunset. Then, after dark, we'll venture out to eat.

John is saying, "Only four more days till we hit the end of the pipeline. Try and get us a job in the mountains, Pops. This sand country in July is too much like work."

"I'll see what I can do, John." As I duck into the pickup's shaded cab, I add, "Yes, the high country *would* be nice."

From the truck I can see all that we have surveyed today, and my eyes follow the pipeline. The fluttering chain of blue and orange flags stretches from horizon to horizon under an endless turquoise sky.

Chapin Grayware water jar—Northern Anasazi. Drawing by Scott Andrae.

Cliff dwellings. Drawing by Scott Andrae.

INDEX

112

DAVID EDWARD STUART has been in love with anthropology most of his life. Although he has conducted field work in Alaska, Mexico, and South America, he fell in love with New Mexico and the state's rich heritage during the 1960s. Awarded the Ph.D. by the University of New Mexico in 1972, he taught briefly in Florida before returning to U.N.M. as a founding staff-member of the Office of Contract Archeology.

Since 1977, Dr. Stuart has been a consulting anthropologist in Albuquerque--the only independent anthropologist honored with a biography in *Who's Who in the World*. Between assignments he has authored more than one hundred publications and is best known for his textbook, *Prehistoric New Mexico*, and for his "New Mexico's Heritage" newspaper series.

David lives near the University, keeps "writer's hours" when not on assignment, and enjoys meeting friends in coffee shops to talk about anthropology, public affairs, and writing. He occasionally teaches an evening course, "Ancient Man in New Mexico," at the University of New Mexico.